France

France

BY DON NARDO

Enchantment of the World
Second Series

Children's Press®

A Division of Grolier Publishing

NEW YORK   LONDON   HONG KONG   SYDNEY
DANBURY, CONNECTICUT

Frontispiece: Lavender in bloom

Consultant: Ioannis Sinanoglou, Ph.D., Executive Director, Council for European Studies, Columbia University

Please note: All statistics are as up-to-date as possible at the time of publication.

Visit Children's Press on the Internet: http://publishing.grolier.com

Book production by Herman Adler Design Group

Library of Congress Cataloging-in-Publication Data

Nardo, Don, 1947–
     France / by Don Nardo.
         p. cm. — (Enchantment of the world. Second series)
     Includes bibliographical references and index.
     Summary: Describes the geography, plants and animals, history, economy, language, sports, arts, religions, culture, and people of France.
     ISBN 0-516-21052-1
     1. France—Juvenile literature. [1. France.] I. Title. II. Series.
DC17.N37 2000
944—dc21   99-12685
                                                                                                  CIP

© 2000 by Children's Press®, a Division of Grolier Publishing Co., Inc.
   2 3 4 5 6 7 8 9 10 R 09 08 07 06 05 04 03 02 01 00

France

Contents

Cover photo:
Paris by night

The Tour de France

Rodin's *The Thinker*

France's Patriotic Spirit Is Born

I N A VERY REAL WAY, THE MODERN NATION OF FRANCE AND its patriotic spirit came into being on July 16 and 17 in the year 1429. The scene was the town of Reims, at that time the traditional site where the French crowned their kings. For some seventeen years, France had been torn asunder by a bloody civil war. And Reims had long been under the control of the Burgundians, one of the country's two warring factions. The Burgundians were allied with the English, who occupied much of France and claimed the exclusive right to rule it.

Opposing the Burgundians and the English were other French—the Armagnacs—who wanted France to be a free and independent nation. The Armagnacs set up a rival court and fortified stronghold at Chinon, in central France. Year

Opposite: **A triumphant Joan of Arc entering the town of Orléans in 1429**

Joan of Arc first met Charles VII at the château of Chinon.

Charles VII entering Paris

after year they desperately struggled to liberate the many French towns under enemy control.

The Armagnac leader, Charles VII, was the rightful heir to the French throne. His father, Charles VI, who had died in 1422, had been officially crowned the French king at Reims. But the younger Charles could not claim the throne until he too was crowned in a splendid ceremony in that city. The English and Burgundians, fearing that as king Charles might inspire and strengthen the Armagnacs' cause, had long kept him from reaching Reims.

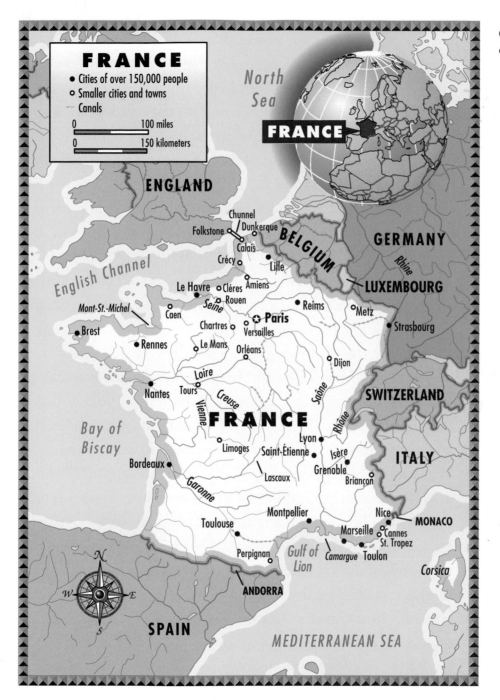

FRANCE

- Cities of over 150,000 people
- Smaller cities and towns
- Canals

0   100 miles

0   150 kilometers

FRANCE

North
Sea

ENGLAND

English Channel

GERMANY

BELGIUM

LUXEMBOURG

Chunnel
Folkstone
Dunkerque
Calais
Crécy
Lille
Rhine

Le Havre
Cléres
Amiens
Seine
Rouen
Reims
Metz
Strasbourg

Mont-St.-Michel
Caen
Chartres
Paris
Versailles

Brest
Rennes
Le Mans
Orléans
Dijon

Loire
Nantes
Tours
Creuse
Vienne
FRANCE
Saône
SWITZERLAND

Bay of
Biscay

Rhône

Limoges
Lyon
ITALY

Saint-Étienne
Isère
Grenoble
Bordeaux
Lascaux
Briançon

Garonne

Montpellier
Nice
MONACO

Toulouse
Marseille
Cannes
St. Tropez

Perpignan
Camargue
Toulon
Corsica

Gulf of
Lion

ANDORRA

SPAIN

MEDITERRANEAN SEA

All of this changed, however, in July 1429. On the fourteenth or fifteenth of that month, the Burgundian soldiers in charge of Reims fled when they heard that Charles VII and his new "champion" were approaching at the head of an army. That champion was a seventeen-year-old girl named Jeanne d'Arc, known to us as Joan of Arc. She claimed that she had recently heard the voices of angels and long-dead Christian saints. The voices, she said, had instructed her to put on armor and liberate the town of Orléans, to which the English had laid siege with thousands of troops. Charles had accepted her story and had given her command of an army. And by May 8, 1429, after several furious battles, she had driven the enemy away from Orléans, saving the city.

During the following two months, Joan's army had marched northward toward Reims, winning more victories along the way. Finally, on July 16, Charles and Joan entered Reims in triumph. All the town's inhabitants gathered in the streets and town square, loudly cheering and celebrating their liberation. They were awed and thrilled at the unusual sight of a young woman decked out in shining armor, riding a handsome white horse, and carrying a magnificent banner bearing images of Jesus and the archangels Michael and Gabriel. The next day—July 17, 1429—Joan proudly knelt beside Charles in the crowded local cathedral. There, a French clergyman crowned him Charles VII, the "Lord's anointed," the legitimate king of France.

After the coronation, Joan's personal fortunes changed for the worse. She was captured in battle and held prisoner by the

*Joan of Arc Led to Her
Execution* by Isidor Patrois

Burgundians and English. They accused her of being a witch, put her on trial, and on May 30, 1431, burned her at the stake. But the revolution she and Charles had set in motion could not be stopped. Inspired by her example and sacrifice, the Armagnacs fought on, won victory after victory, and prevailed. In 1435, they signed a treaty with the Burgundians, ending the civil war. Led by Charles, now the undisputed king, united French armies then drove the English completely out of the country by 1453. Joan of Arc was declared a saint in 1920. Ever since her victory in 1429, France has been fiercely patriotic and proud of its heritage, culture, and unity, forged over the centuries by kings, emperors, and republican revolutionaries.

CHAPTER

TWO

A Miniature Version of Europe

14

M<small>ODERN</small> F<small>RANCE IS SHAPED ALMOST LIKE A HEXAGON,</small> a six-sided figure. That hexagon covers 212,918 square miles (551,415 sq km), including the French island of Corsica off the country's southeastern coast. The six sides of the French hexagon enclose an area almost as big as the U.S. state of Texas, making France the largest country in western Europe. In fact, France stretches about 590 miles (950 km) from the picturesque beaches of Calais and Dunkirk on the English

Opposite: **The Dordogne Valley in the Aquitaine region**

Seaside cliffs along France's northern coast

Snow-capped peaks in the Pyrenees

Channel to its southernmost tip in the rugged Pyrenees—a 270-mile (435-km)-long chain of mountains that marks the border with Spain and the small Principality of Andorra.

Spain is not the only country that shares a border with France. The eastern side of the French hexagon touches Italy, Switzerland, and Germany, while the northeastern side faces the small nations of Luxembourg and Belgium. The hexagon's other sides border the Atlantic Ocean and the Mediterranean Sea.

The Paris Basin

France is not only the largest western European country, but it also has a tremendous diversity of geographical features and climates. Some experts call the country a microcosm—a miniature version—of Europe because it has all three of the major kinds of landforms found in Europe. The first of these

The Chunnel

Throughout most of history, France and England could not be said to border each other because they were separated by the English Channel. This changed, however, with the 1994 opening of the *Tunnel sous La Manche*, known in English as the Channel Tunnel. Nicknamed the "Chunnel," the underwater structure has two railway lines that link Calais, in northern France, to Folkestone, in southern England. The ride takes about thirty-five minutes, while ferry service across the Channel takes several hours. Using the Chunnel, a person can leave Paris at 9:00 A.M. and reach London, over 200 miles (322 km) away, by noon.

are the relatively flat lowland basins that make up the valleys of the Loire, Seine, Rhône, and Garonne Rivers. Over the ages, the rivers have deposited enormous amounts of sediments, creating an abundance of rich farmland in these basins.

A vineyard in the rich farmland of the Rhône Valley

France's population is concentrated in the Paris Basin.

The largest, most productive, and most famous of France's lowland basins is the Paris Basin, in the nation's north-central sector. This huge, saucer-shaped region, with Paris near its center, covers about 39,000 square miles (100,000 sq km)—about one-fifth of France's entire area. Throughout history, the bulk of the nation's population has been concentrated here.

It is easy to see why people have always been so attracted to the Paris Basin. For one thing, it has an extremely pleasant climate. The winters are cool, but rarely cold, and the summers are long and warm. The average temperature across north-central France in July is a comfortable 75°F (24°C). More importantly, the thick, fertile soil in the region favors the production of grains, fruits, and other crops, as well as the raising of cattle, pigs, and other livestock. In addition, most of the country's industry and economic activity is located in the Paris Basin. The combination of all these factors explains why the region attracts and maintains as much as 25 percent of the country's entire population.

France's Geographical Features

Land Area (including the island of Corsica): 212,918 square miles (551,415 sq km)

Largest City: Paris

Highest Elevation: Mont Blanc, 15,771 feet (4,807 m), in the French Alps

Lowest Elevation: Sections of the delta of the Rhône River that are slightly below sea level.

Longest River: Loire, 634 miles (1,020 km)

Largest Lake: Lac du Bourget, in east-central France, 16.6 square miles (43 sq km)

Total Length of Coastlines (including Corsica): 2,300 miles (3,700 km)

Highest Average Temperature: Nice (on Mediterranean coast), 81°F (27°C), in July

Lowest Average Temperature: Briançon (in French Alps), 28°F (-2°C), in January

Looking at French Cities

With a population of about 422,000 people, Lyon (above, left) is France's third-largest city. It lies 287 miles (462 km) southeast of Paris, in the lush Rhône-Saône Corridor near the point where these two major rivers meet. Lyon is a very ancient city. The Romans made it the capital of their province of Gaul in the 40s B.C., and its name comes from a Latin word meaning "Hill of the Crow." The city still has many ancient houses and buildings. Among these are the Church of Ainay, dating from the fourth century, and the Choristers' House, built in the tenth century. And still visible are a number of *traboules*—secret passages dug underneath buildings, which French freedom fighters used to evade the Nazis during World War II. Today's residents are also proud of the city's more modern aspects. Perhaps most prominent among these is *Presqu'île* (Almost Island), a 6-mile (10-km)-long fingerlike peninsula between the rivers. The district is crowded with excellent shops, restaurants, museums, and theaters.

The fifth-largest French city, Nice, with more than 345,000 people, rests near the eastern end of the lovely Côte d'Azur—the French Riviera—on the Mediterranean coast. Its warm weather, averaging a toasty 81°F (27°C) in July and a pleasant 55°F (13°C) in January, attracts tens of thousands of visitors a year. Many relax and sunbathe on the beaches (above, right) or stroll among the palm trees. At night, gambling in the city's casinos is popular. Another attraction is *Vieux Nice* (Old Nice), a network of quaint alleyways lined with seventeenth- and eighteenth-century buildings. For many visitors, the highlight of the Vieux Nice is a romantic cliff fortress, the *Colline du Château* (Castle Hill), which was first inhabited more than 2,000 years ago.

Bordeaux (below), with a population of just over 200,000, is the eighth-largest city in France. Located in a strategic position near the mouth of the busy Garonne River, the city is also the country's second-biggest seaport, after Marseille. Like so many other French cities, Bordeaux is very old. Among its attractions are the ruins of a Roman amphitheater, where gladiators once fought to the death. The city also has a cathedral erected about the year 1100 and an elegant theater inaugurated in 1780. Not far from this landmark stretches the *Esplanade des Quinconces*, the largest town square in all of Europe. Although shipping is a major local industry, Bordeaux is best known for its fine wines. The region surrounding the city is filled with rich vineyards.

France has several other lowland basins and gently rolling plains, each dominated by a major river system. One of these, the Alsace Plain, lies east of the Paris Basin along the Rhine River, which forms the boundary between France and its neighbor Germany. The Alsace region is renowned for its grapes, which are used to make fine wines, especially white wines.

Another basin, the Aquitaine, lies along the Atlantic coast southwest of the Paris Basin. The peaceful Garonne River meanders through the beautiful Aquitaine lowlands, which feature alternating patches of lush rolling farmland and shady groves of pine trees. This region too is known for its wine grapes, particularly around Bordeaux, a small city located near the mouth of the Garonne.

Because the Aquitaine borders the ocean, it benefits from the warming effect of the mild Gulf Stream waters that flow nearby. This provides the region with a temperate climate characterized by mild winters and somewhat cool but still pleasant summers. This maritime climate extends up the coast into the region known as Brittany, which protrudes like a huge thumb out into the Atlantic. The city of Brest, on Brittany's western coast, averages 45°F (7°C) in January and 61°F (16°C) in July.

More than 100 miles (161 km) east of the Aquitaine lowlands lies a longer and narrower but very fertile valley—the Rhône-Saône Corridor. This valley stretches north-to-south for more than 250 miles (402 km) along the Rhône and Saône Rivers. In the heart of the valley, amid green plains dotted by fruit orchards, vegetable gardens, and vineyards, stands Lyon, France's third-largest city. Not surprisingly, Lyon has numerous facilities for processing and packing these crops. The moist lowlands of the Rhône's delta are in the southernmost section of the Rhône-Saône Corridor.

The Sky Blue Coast

The French call the region lying just east of the Rhône delta the *Côte d'Azur*, or "Sky Blue Coast." Many foreigners know the area as the French Riviera, a world-famous vacation spot. Both local and foreign tourists are attracted to the Côte d'Azur's extremely pleasant climate. The region borders the warm waters of the Mediterranean Sea, and so enjoys what geographers and weather experts call a Mediterranean

The rocky coastline of Saint-Raphaël on the Côte d'Azur

climate, with hot dry summers and mild humid winters. For instance, in the city of Marseille, on the coast southeast of the delta, the average temperature is 45°F (7°C) in January and 73°F (23°C) in July. Marseille receives about 22 inches (56 cm) of rainfall on about sixty days a year. The sun shines most of the rest of the time.

This almost ideal climate prevails along the coast stretching eastward from Marseille, including the famous resort towns of Toulon, Saint-Tropez, Cannes, and Nice. All boast beautiful beaches frequented by sunbathers. Cannes is also renowned for its yearly film festival, which attracts movie stars from around the world. Nice, a few miles east of Cannes, enjoys the warmest average temperature in France—81°F (27°C) in July.

The Highland Plateaus

France's second major landform is its highland plateaus, rugged rocky regions rising to a few hundred or thousand feet above sea level. These are the remnants of ancient mountain ranges that wind, rain, and sun have eroded, or worn down, over millions of years. Large portions of these regions are wild, difficult to traverse, and only sparsely inhabited. Typical terrain consists of steep, jagged hillsides and ravines dotted with small trees, bushes, and other meager vegetation.

The largest highland plateau in France is the Massif Central. Sandwiched between the Aquitaine Basin and the Rhône-Saône Valley, and occupying most of south-central France, it covers some 33,000 square miles (85,000 sq km).

The plateau's outer fringes are less than 1,000 feet (305 m) high, but much of the central portion rises to between 5,000 and 6,000 feet (1,520–1,830 m). Its masses of rugged cliffs, gorges, and other rocky formations have inspired some writers to call this region France's "central natural fortress."

The climate in most of the Massif Central is not nearly as mild and temperate as the climates in the valleys or along the coasts. Summers are moderately warm, averaging about 66°F (19°C), but shorter than summers in the lowlands. Sudden—and often very destructive—thunderstorms whip across the plateau in the summer. By contrast, winters are cold, averaging about 30°F (-1°C). The region is often blanketed by deep snows that can block passes and roads for several months, making it difficult or impossible to reach remote areas.

When these snows melt in the spring, they feed the plateau's network of hundreds of small, winding mountain streams. These streams converge to form the sources for several of France's major rivers, including the Loire and the Vienne.

Because of its difficult terrain and sometimes harsh climate, the Massif Central has few sizable towns or major roads. Many of the existing roads zigzag through the bottoms of chasms or snake back and forth along the sides of steep hills or cliffs. Driving these routes can be a frightening experience, especially when only a few inches of pavement separate your car from a

This road winds through the steep hillsides of the Massif Central.

Mountains Rise and Fall

The massive highland plateau known as the Massif Central was once a lofty range of mountains like today's Alps. The Massif Central and France's other rocky plateaus were formed more than 300 million years ago in what scientists call the Paleozoic Era. About 190 million years ago, in the Mesozoic Era, some of these ranges were partially submerged under water as surrounding sea levels rose. This flooding, combined with the effects of rain, wind, and temperature extremes, eventually wore down the old mountains, producing the crumbling mixture of cliffs and chasms that make up the plateaus. Meanwhile, the younger Alps and Pyrenees rose in the last 60 million years to form the eastern and southern boundaries of what is now France.

sheer drop-off of hundreds of feet! Yet at the same time, the view from the top of the cliffs is often breathtaking.

The rugged, rocky nature of the plateau's terrain also makes farming difficult. Here and there, in small sheltered valleys nestled between huge boulders and cliffs, villagers tend small crops of corn and vegetables or raise sheep and goats. But these are not large-scale enterprises, as they are in the more fertile river valleys, which export a great deal of food to other parts of France and Europe. Most of the food produced on the plateau is consumed by the local inhabitants.

France's other highland plateaus are a good deal smaller than the Massif Central and have lower elevations so their terrain is less rugged and their climates are less harsh. The

Armorican Massif is located in the northwestern part of the country, west of the Paris Basin, while the Ardennes plateau lies along the borders of Belgium and Luxembourg (most of the plateau is actually in those nations). Still another mountainous plateau, the relatively small Vosges, lies in eastern France between the Paris Basin and the Alsace lowlands.

The Roof of France

The third major type of European landform in France consists of relatively new mountain ranges. These are the Pyrenees and the French Alps. Because they are relatively young as mountains go, nature has not yet had time to wear them down. So these mountains retain many spectacular peaks that soar above the country's plateaus and river valleys. These mountains form, in a sense, the roof of France.

The Pyrenees run east to west along France's southern border with Spain, forming an imposing natural barrier between the two nations. The range features numerous snow-covered peaks, several exceeding 10,000 feet (3,000 m) in height. It has almost no low-lying passes. In fact, there is not a single pass below 5,000 feet (1,524 m) in the range's entire 190-mile (306-km)-long central section. That makes these mountains very difficult to cross.

Stone farm buildings in the Pyrenees

Mont Blanc rises above this mountain village in the Alps.

The French Alps, which rise between France and Italy and Switzerland, also have many towering peaks. The largest of all is Mont Blanc, the tallest mountain in western Europe, which soars to 15,771 feet (4,807 m). Unlike the Pyrenees, the French Alps are broken in places by river valleys, including the Rhône, Isère, and Durance. These provide fairly easy access to Italy and Switzerland, except when the high passes are blocked by snow.

The climate in these mountain chains is generally cold and harsh. Even in the high mountain valleys, where scattered villages and towns are located, winters are long and cold and summers short and cool. The town of Briançon, in the Alps near the Italian border, is typical. The average January temperature in the town is 28°F (-2°C), while in midsummer the thermometer rarely goes above 63°F (17°C). Towns in these high valleys often experience moderate-to-heavy snowfall on fifty or more days a year.

Wildlife Shaped by Human Impact

BECAUSE FRANCE HAS A VARIETY OF LANDSCAPES, RANGING from river valleys and seacoasts to forests, rocky plateaus, and mountain peaks, it supports a wide variety of *flora* (plants) and *fauna* (animals). The country is home to about 100 species of mammals, 50 species of reptiles and amphibians, and more than 300 species of birds. There are also thousands of species of trees, bushes, vines, and other plants—some wild and others cultivated.

It would be a mistake, though, to call these various plant and animal species "French." After all, plants and animals seeking habitats do not recognize political borders, and most of the species found in France are found throughout much of Europe. The kinds, numbers, and distribution of these flora and fauna, however, are not the same today as they were in the past. A few of the changes were caused by natural forces, such as mountain-building and changes in climate. But human intervention has had by far the largest impact on the species, numbers, and habitats of France's plants and animals.

Opposite: **Wild horses of the Camargue**

European bison once roamed the forests of France.

How People Changed France's Environment

Thousands of years ago, France was a natural wonderland of dense forests filled with a wide variety of plants and animals. Huge bison, aurochs (wild oxen), and lynx (large wildcats) roamed through giant stands of beech and oak

A red deer stag running through snow

trees. Large numbers of beavers made their homes in sparkling streams where herds of red deer and wild boar stopped to drink. And thousands of species of wild birds nested in every natural niche, from the verdant marshes of the Rhône delta to the rocky crags and ravines of the Massif Central.

Between 3,000 and 4,000 years ago, when human beings began settling the area on a large scale, the numbers and kinds of both flora and fauna began to change. This was partly because people hunted many animals for food or to use their skins for clothing. In time, such hunting drove the bison, aurochs, and many other large animals to extinction. Others, including the red deer and wild boar, suffered such severe reduction in numbers that they are nearly extinct in France today.

Human settlers also cleared some of the forests for firewood and to build farms and towns. On the one hand, this destroyed or reduced the size of the natural habitats of many animal species. With fewer trees to nest in, for example, many types of birds became more scarce or migrated to other parts of Europe. And human populations increasingly encroached on or polluted the streams and rivers inhabited by beavers. At one time, beavers were plentiful in most of France's lowlands and plateaus. Today, a very small beaver population, protected by law, exists in the Rhône River's tributaries and marshes.

On the other hand, when people cleared the forests they permanently changed the nature of the land and the flora that thrived there. Many of the lowlands and plains were covered by thick forests dominated by shade-loving beech trees. When people began cutting down these trees, more light entered the wooded areas. Over time, this caused a drop in the number of beech trees and an increase in the number of oaks, which can tolerate more direct sunlight. People also introduced herds of grazing animals, such as sheep and goats. Centuries of over-grazing turned many once-green forests into open pastures and heath—treeless areas with poor soil.

Grazing animals such as goats have contributed to the deforestation of France.

France's Shrinking Forests

Long ago, before humans began cutting down trees to make room for towns and farmland, most of France was carpeted by forests. The trees were mostly beeches and oaks, except in the mountains, where firs predominated, and in the temperate southeast, which featured a mixture of pines and oaks. Long after people first settled the area, deforestation, or tree removal, remained small-scale, even in Roman times. The country's most intense periods of deforestation occurred later—between about 950 and 1250, then in the 1400s, the late 1700s, and throughout the 1800s. Today, France's forests cover an estimated 50,000 square miles (129,000 sq km), less than 25 percent of the country's total area.

National Parks and Nature Preserves

Eventually, like people in other countries, the French began to recognize the importance of preserving the natural environment. Major and effective efforts to do so were a long time coming, however. Royal edicts designed to protect the forests were issued in 1219, 1515, and 1669, but these did little in the short run—and nothing in the long run—to stop the destruction of trees. In 1853 a group of French painters called on the government to create a nature preserve to protect plants and animals. And in 1901 a few concerned French citizens formed a society dedicated to protecting the country's natural heritage.

But it was not until the 1960s that the French government began to protect plants and animals on a large scale. In 1966, most of the nation's forests came under the protection of the *Office National des Forêts* (National Forest Service). And in

1971, the government created the official organization that later became known as the *Ministère de l'Environnement et du Cadre de Vie* (Ministry for the Environment and the Quality of Life).

In the meantime, the government began setting aside small portions of the country as national parks and nature preserves. The national parks are designed to maintain large tracts of land in their present state, so that both French citizens and visitors can appreciate what remains of the nation's natural heritage. The first national park, the Vanoise, covering about 208 square miles (539 sq km) in the French Alps, came into being in 1963. By 1979, five more national parks had been created.

A visitor to the Vanoise National Park encounters some permanent residents.

During the 1960s and 1970s, France also witnessed the creation of many small nature preserves. These are designed to protect specific kinds of flora and fauna that are rare or in danger of becoming extinct. The largest nature preserve in France is the Étang de Vaccarès, which covers about 39 square miles (101 sq km) in the Camargue, the Rhône River's marshy delta. The area is a vital habitat for beavers, badgers, and more

The Protected Lands of the Camargue

The Camargue is the large, marshy delta of the Rhône River. Its rich soil, which supports a lush cover of grasses, bushes, flowers, and other plants, was formed by the river as it laid down sediments over thousands of years. In the past, herds of wild horses and black bulls roamed the area. Today, small surviving populations of both species are bred and maintained by the government and local rancher/cowboys known as *gardians*. Part of the Camargue became a protected area, the Étang de Vaccarès preserve, in 1970. Among the protected flora is the *saladelle*, a blue flower the *gardians* have adopted as their symbol. Among the many birds protected in the preserve are wild ducks, egrets, herons, and flamingos (above). In fact, the Camargue is the only known nesting area in Europe for flamingos, beautiful long-legged wading birds native to Africa and Asia.

than 200 species of birds. Among the country's numerous other nature preserves is the *Sept-Îles* (Seven Islands), a group of tiny islands off the coast of Brittany. Some of these islands are sanctuaries for nesting gulls, cormorants, puffins, gannets, oystercatchers, and other birds.

Human Inhabitants of the Parks

Overall, France's six national parks and eighty-three nature parks and preserves cover about 8 percent of the country. Foreign tourists are often surprised to find people living in these protected zones. This is especially true of Americans and Canadians, who are accustomed to their own vast, uninhabited national parks, such as Yellowstone National Park in Wyoming, Idaho, and Montana. However, France is much smaller and far older than the United States and Canada, and there are almost no completely uninhabited areas left (mountain peaks being an obvious exception). Tourists are also impressed by how carefully the human residents of France's nature parks and preserves follow the rules and restrictions set down to protect the wildlife.

Common Plants and Animals

Outside of the nature preserves and zoos, the type and distribution of France's plants and animals have been determined largely by the needs of humans. For instance, a large portion of the country's lowlands is farmland, so wheat, corn, grapevines, and other crops are the most common plants outside of the remaining forests. Most other unforested areas in the lowlands consist of grassy pastures or heath created by tree removal.

Soil quality, rainfall, temperature, and altitude are among the factors that determine which trees and bushes predominate in the forests or in small stands scattered through the French countryside. Oak and beech are most common across the lowlands of northern and central France. Hornbeam, a

French Zoos

The most exotic of France's wild animals are imported from other lands and exhibited in spacious, well-managed zoos called *parcs zoologiques* (animal parks). One of the most popular, the Parc Zoologique des Minières at Doué-la-Fontaine in the Loire Valley, features deer, monkeys, and emu (large, flightless birds native to Australia). The Parc Zoologique de Cléres, in Normandy, has antelopes, kangaroos, monkeys, and more than 750 species of birds.

Larger wild beasts, including elephants, hippos, camels, zebras, and lions, can be seen in the zoo in Thoiry, a few miles west of Paris. This fascinating facility also features the world's first "ligrons," a cross between a lion and a tiger.

The Western Desman

Nicknamed the "water mole" because it spends much of its time in streams and ponds, the western desman lives only in the Pyrenees Mountains in southern France and northern Spain. Its scientific name is *Galemys pyrenaicus*. The average adult desman is about 11 inches (28 cm) long, counting its scaly tail. It uses its long snout to scoop up its favorite food—insects.

sturdy small tree in the birch family, frequently grows beneath the foliage of the larger oak. In the west and southwest, stands of oak and sweet chestnut are found amid large stretches of heath, while the southern Atlantic shore features forests of maritime pine. Higher altitudes, including sections of the Massif Central, Pyrenees, and Alps, have silver fir, spruce, Scotch pine, and larch. In the warm Mediterranean climate of the southeast, cork oak, kermes oak, Aleppo pine, and olive trees thrive.

Olive trees (foreground) thrive in the southeast.

Domestic livestock are the most common and numerous animals in France. The country contains about 220 million chickens and other poultry, for example. It also has over 23 million cattle, 12 million pigs, 11 million sheep, 1 million goats, and several hundred thousand horses.

Apart from insects and birds, France's most common wild animals are small mammals, reptiles, and amphibians found in many parts of Europe, as well as in Asia and North America. These include mice, rats, squirrels, and other rodents, as well as lizards and snakes. The only mammal native to France is the western desman, a kind of mole.

Many geese are raised on farms in France.

Cattle at pasture in Brittany

A History Shaped by Many Peoples

THE NATION-STATE OF FRANCE DID NOT BEGIN TO DEVELOP until late medieval times. Yet the land that is now France has been inhabited by humans for thousands of years. Each of the many peoples who occupied the area left its mark, its customs and values helping to shape the country's culture and national character.

Opposite: **Charlemagne ruled France from 768 to 814.**

The first people to inhabit what is now France were stone-age hunters, the Neanderthals. Evidence gathered by archaeologists—scientists who study the ruins and artifacts of past civilizations—suggests that tribes of Neanderthals lived in the region at least 70,000 years ago. Short, stocky, and physically strong, they were hunter-gatherers who used tools made of stone and animal bones. During cold weather, they camped in caves. There, they built fires to cook their meat and scare off wild animals.

Sometime between 40,000 and 30,000 B.C., another race of humans arrived in France. They are called Cro-Magnons after the cave of that name in southern France where archaeologists first discovered their remains in 1868. Like the Neanderthals, the Cro-Magnons were hunter-gatherers who roamed from place to place, following migrating herds and changing animal populations. But the Cro-Magnons apparently were more advanced and efficient hunters than the Neanderthals. Animal bones found at Cro-Magnon sites reveal that they regularly stalked and killed large beasts,

The Lascaux Cave Paintings

In 1940, four teenage boys playing in the forest found the entrance to a cave. When they climbed inside with lanterns, they were astonished to see many large and colorful paintings on the cave's walls. Archaeologists explored the site and found more than 600 paintings in all, as well as almost 1,500 engravings carved into the walls. Scholars think these treasures were created by Cro-Magnon artists about 17,000 years ago. The cave was opened to the public in 1948, but it was closed in 1963 because the visitors' breath and body heat were damaging the paintings.

In 1983, an exact replica of the cave and its artworks, Lascaux II, opened. It thrills thousands of visitors from around the world each year.

including mammoths (huge, hairy elephants), reindeer, and horses. The Cro-Magnons also produced art in the form of magnificent cave paintings. The most impressive known examples came to light in 1940 at Lascaux in the Aquitaine region, east of Bordeaux.

Waves of Outsiders, from Hunters to Farmers

The hunter-gatherer societies living in France changed very little in the course of thousands of years. Then, about 4000 B.C. new nomadic tribes arrived in the area, bringing with them knowledge of how to grow crops and raise livestock. This knowledge was revolutionary. Combined with hunting, it provided people with a much more reliable food supply than they could get by hunting and gathering alone. Now they were able to settle down and create farms and villages. Another technical advance occurred about 2000 B.C., when a new wave of outsiders entered the French hexagon. This group introduced metal tools and weapons, which proved to be much more efficient than those made of stone.

Between 1000 and 750 B.C., tribal peoples calling themselves Celts migrated to France from central Europe. The Celts were considerably more advanced than the natives already inhabiting the area. In addition to sheep, cattle, and other domesticated animals, the Celts had horses, which they used for riding and for pulling carts. They also had knowledge of the wheel and used iron tools and weapons. Celtic civilization spread throughout France and began to diversify. By the first century B.C., more than 200 separate tribes lived in the area, each with its own customs and territory, often including towns with strong defensive walls.

The handle and scabbard of a Celtic bronze dagger

This Celtic helmet is decorated with elaborate designs and ornamentation.

The Greeks in France

A group of settlers from the Greek city-state of Phocaea landed at the site of modern Marseille, on France's southern coast, about 600 B.C. The city they founded was then called Massilia. It did not take long for the enterprising Greeks to develop a thriving trade with some of the Celtic tribes living to the north. Greek artifacts made in 500 B.C. have been found almost as far north as Paris. The Greeks introduced new farming techniques and religious ideas, and also the cultivation of grapevines, laying the foundation for the French wine industry.

The Romans Conquer France

Shortly before the start of the first century B.C., the Romans began making inroads into France. They referred to the region as "Gaul" and called the Celts "Gauls." By this time, the Romans, who came from central Italy, had carved out a huge empire that included nearly all the lands bordering the Mediterranean Sea. Unlike the scattered Gallic (Celtic) tribes, who had no central government or national army, Rome was a well-organized nation with a large and brutally efficient army.

In 118 B.C., the Romans established a colony on France's southern coast, about 120 miles (193 km) west of the Greek city of Massilia. Greek settlers in the area had long been content to remain on the coast and, except for exchanging trade goods, left the Gauls alone. But the Romans were obsessed with expanding their empire and their influence. Soon, the Roman colony expanded into a large province, the Narbonese (or Narbonensis).

The Roman intrusion into Gaul became a full-blown conquest about a half-century later. In 58 B.C., the renowned Roman leader Julius Caesar marched

Julius Caesar

northward from the Narbonese at the head of his army. Over the next six years, Caesar subdued the Gallic tribes one by one, laying waste to villages, farms, and entire cultures. In all, he fought over thirty major battles, captured more than 800 towns, and killed more than a million Gauls.

After they had conquered Gaul, the Romans vigorously began "Romanizing" the remaining Gauls. They taught them to speak Latin and to adopt Roman customs and ideas, including concepts of law and statecraft. Meanwhile, thousands of Romans settled in Gaul and, over time, intermarried with the natives. They divided the country into several new provinces and built cities, roads, aqueducts, temples, amphitheaters, and bathhouses. Roman ideas and customs took firm root in the area and profoundly shaped the development of French culture.

France's First Hero

By the end of 53 B.C., Julius Caesar thought his conquest of Gaul was over. But he was wrong. Early in 52 B.C., a defiant chief of the Arverni tribe, which inhabited the northern part of the Massif Central, launched a bloody rebellion against the Romans. This shrewd and capable military leader, named Vercingetorix, gathered warriors from many tribes and fought the Roman army almost to a standstill. He finally had to surrender to Caesar (left) when most of his allies abandoned his cause, but his courage and ability were never forgotten. In modern times, the French proclaimed Vercingetorix a national hero and erected statues in his honor.

The Coming of the Franks

For several centuries, Gaul thrived as part of the Roman Empire. In the fifth century A.D., however, that empire fell apart as numerous nomadic tribes, much like the original Celts, swept across Europe in search of new living space. Among the new peoples who passed through or settled Gaul were the Visigoths, Vandals, and Burgundians, but the most important were the Franks, who gave their name to the area. In the late 400s, a Frank named Clovis set up the Frankish Kingdom—*regnum Francorum* in Latin. Over time, *Francorum* became *Francia* and finally *France*.

Clovis established the Frankish Kingdom in the late 400s. He is shown here receiving the fleur-de-lis from an angel.

Clovis established the French Merovingian dynasty, or ruling family line, named for his grandfather, Merowen (or Merovech). Because Clovis converted to Christianity, his realm became Christian and has remained so ever since. He made Paris his capital city, helping to establish its long-term importance. When Clovis died in 511, his four sons divided the kingdom among themselves. They and the leaders of the next several generations of Merovingians fought almost continuous civil wars, each attempting to gain control of the whole country for themselves.

By the late 600s and early 700s, the Merovingian rulers had become so corrupt and weak that they lost the reins of power to their chief advisors. These were the Carolingians, who soon established their own dynasty. In 732, a Carolingian named Charles Martel saved France, and probably all of Europe as well, from conquest. Near Tours, in west-central France, he defeated a large army of Muslims who had earlier crossed over from North Africa and taken control of Spain. They were now bent on subjugating France.

Martel's grandson, Charlemagne, engaged in even more ambitious military campaigns. In only a few years he secured an empire that included not only France, but also parts of what are now Belgium, Germany, and Italy. In the year 800, Pope Leo III crowned him emperor of what Charlemagne and many others believed was a reborn Roman Empire. But this lofty dream came to nothing. After Charlemagne died in 814, his descendants fought among themselves, as Clovis's heirs had. They carved the empire up into their own petty kingdoms, and it slowly but steadily fell apart.

Some Famous Carolingian Rulers and Their Reigns	
Pepin the Short	751–768
Charlemagne	768–814
Louis I	814–840
Charles the Bald	843–877
Charles the Fat	884–887
Charles the Simple	893–923

Carolingian Empires

Kingdom of the Franks 768

Farthest extent of Charlemagne's empire

Partition of Verdun 843

During the reign of one of the last Carolingian rulers, Charles the Simple, the seeds of a long rivalry between France and England were planted. Bands of Norsemen (Vikings) from what are now Norway and Denmark had long been raiding

Norse ships arriving at Paris

northern France. Eventually, the Norsemen sailed up the Seine River and attacked Paris. In 911, the frightened Charles made a deal with their leader, Rollo, giving him the region in northwestern France that was and still is called Normandy. Its people subsequently became known as Normans.

In the years that followed, the Normans transformed their small territory into a prosperous and powerful state. Although it was physically part of France, it became more or less a separate kingdom in its own right. In 1066, a descendant of Rollo, William I, crossed the English Channel, defeated the English at the Battle of

Hastings, and seized control of England. This earned him the nickname of "William the Conqueror." The Norman-English rulers who succeeded him held onto their lands in Normandy and even expanded them at the expense of the French kings.

Friction steadily mounted between France and England. And eventually the French kings, now members of the Capetian dynasty (established in 987), began trying to expel the English from France. Full-scale war broke out in 1337. It became known as the Hundred Years' War, although it lasted a bit longer than a century. Most of the fighting consisted of small-scale raids on enemy towns and villages, although there were a few large battles. In two of these engagements, at Crécy (1346) and Poitiers (1356), the French were caught under

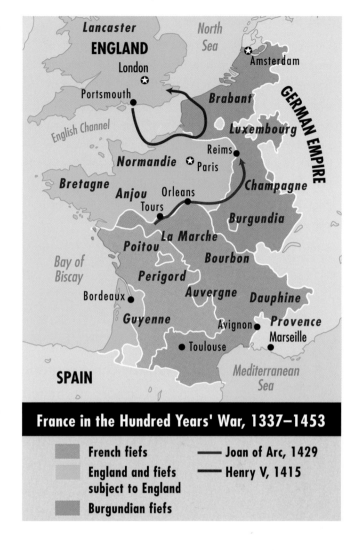

France in the Hundred Years' War, 1337–1453

- French fiefs
- England and fiefs subject to England
- Burgundian fiefs
- —— Joan of Arc, 1429
- —— Henry V, 1415

a blizzard of arrows unleashed by English longbows and suffered huge losses. Over time, though, the French rebounded. The climax of the war came in 1453 when Charles VII succeeded in driving the English out of France. In a sense, this event marked the birth of the French nation-state that would later become the nation of France.

The Slaughter at Crécy

On August 26, 1346, England's King Edward III gathered his army near the village of Crécy, not far from the Somme River in northern France. Of his 14,000 troops, almost 8,000 were archers armed with powerful English longbows. The French, led by King Philip VI, had a considerably larger army. During the fighting, masses of French mounted knights repeatedly charged the English lines, but most were killed or unhorsed by hails of arrows. English soldiers armed with swords and knives then swarmed in and slaughtered the survivors.

France Expands Its Power and Influence

In the three centuries following Charles VII's reign, many of his successors attempted to expand France's power, as well as their own. The French kings increased their own authority by steadily reducing the power of the nobles, who had long ruled their vast estates like petty kingdoms. Some French kings also pursued a vigorous foreign policy. For example, Francis I, who ruled from 1515 to 1547, waged numerous wars in Europe. In these conflicts, he won control of important Italian territories and initiated a long-lasting rivalry between French and German rulers.

Francis also sponsored voyages of exploration to the recently discovered New World. Beginning in 1534, French navigator Jacques Cartier led three expeditions to what is now southern Canada and traveled up the St. Lawrence River. Based on his exploits, the French laid claim to Canada, marking the establishment of France's overseas empire.

Jacques Cartier exploring the Saint Lawrence River in Canada

Louis XIV was known as the "Sun King."

Reign of the Sun King

Perhaps the greatest French king of all was Louis XIV, known as the "Sun King." He ruled from 1643 to 1715, the longest royal reign in European history. Determined to make France the strongest nation on earth, he fought four large-scale wars against other European powers, seized land in Italy and the Netherlands, and set up prosperous trading posts in North America and India. Louis was also a staunch patron of the arts and learning. His government established academies of painting and sculpture, science, architecture, and music. He also transformed a royal hunting lodge into the magnificent Palace of Versailles, near Paris.

Europe's Most Lavish Palace

Louis XIV assigned architect Louis Le Vau to design the new palace at Versailles (about 11 miles [18 km] southwest of Paris) and hired André Le Nôtre to lay out its lavish gardens, which cover 250 acres (101 ha). Some 36,000 workers labored for almost thirty years on the project. In 1682, the king moved into what was at the time the most luxurious royal residence in Europe before it was even completed. When finally finished, the palace was so huge that it contained a chapel, a theater, an opera house, and accommodated over 10,000 guests and servants.

Needless to say, Louis's wars, building projects, and lavish lifestyle were not cheap. Much of the money came from taxing France's commoners, the working people who were collectively known as the "third estate." Most belonged to the lowest—and by far the largest—social class, made up of poor peasants, laborers, and craftsmen. The third estate also contained a smaller number of slightly better-off shopkeepers, businessmen, lawyers, and doctors—the country's middle class. France's second estate consisted of the well-to-do nobility, and the Christian clergy made up the first estate. Members of the first and second estates, who together formed only about 3 percent of the nation's population, did not have to pay taxes, so they enjoyed luxurious lifestyles, largely at the commoners' expense.

The French Revolution

This unfair situation became increasingly unbearable and dangerous in the years following Louis XIV's death. His successor, Louis XV, wasted large sums of money on personal luxuries. He also waged costly wars, the most devastating being the Seven Years' War (called the French and Indian War in the Americas), which lasted from 1756 to 1763. France was defeated and lost most of its overseas empire, including its North American colonies, to Britain.

Louis XV died in 1774 and another weak and selfish king, Louis XVI, took the throne. The commoners continued to bear the burden of heavy taxes, but the national treasury continued to shrink, until in 1787 it was virtually empty and the country was deeply in debt. Social discontent, which had been building for decades, rapidly neared the breaking point.

Then, early in 1789, Louis made the mistake of calling a meeting of delegates from each of the country's three estates. He hoped to squeeze more money out of the third estate. But the plan backfired when its delegates suddenly and boldly declared themselves to be France's National Assembly and demanded that the king draft a new constitution reducing the monarchy's power. When Louis refused, a Paris mob stormed and captured the Bastille, the royal fortress-prison. The date was July 14, 1789, which the French have celebrated as their independence day ever since.

A modern fireworks display on Bastille Day, when the French celebrate their independence

"Let them eat cake"

Marie Antoinette (1755–1793) was an Austrian princess. She married Louis XVI, who was then the crown prince of France, in 1770. She became queen at the death of Louis XV in 1774. Marie Antoinette was beautiful and spirited, but the French people saw her as a selfish spendthrift opposed to political reforms and social justice. When told that the poor had no bread, she supposedly made the heartless reply, "Let them eat cake." Thousands of commoners cheered when she died on the guillotine, executed by the new national government on October 16, 1793.

Over the next ten years, France underwent massive turmoil, bloodshed, and political chaos as the revolution passed through various stages. The new popular government abolished the monarchy and declared France a republic (later called the First Republic) in September 1792. After being tried for treason, Louis was executed four months later. Soon afterward, the government fell into the hands of extremists and thousands of French nobles were beheaded in the "Reign of Terror" that followed. Among them was Louis's wife, Queen Marie Antoinette.

A Series of Destructive Wars

Eventually, the army, led by the powerful general Napoléon Bonaparte, stepped in and restored order. But the price of that order was dictatorship. In 1799, Napoléon took over the government, assuming the title of First Consul, and in 1804 he made himself emperor. Power over a single country was apparently not enough for him, however. Napoléon initiated an aggressive foreign policy and for several years led French armies to victory over the forces of Europe's strongest nations. This resulted in a European empire rivaled only by that of Charlemagne. Finally, in 1815, the allied armies of Britain, Prussia, and Austria defeated Napoléon at Waterloo, in Belgium, and he was exiled to an island in the south Atlantic.

Napoléon's retreat from Waterloo

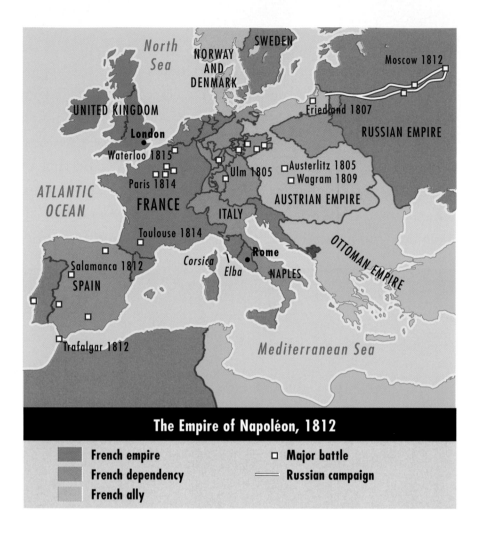

The Empire of Napoléon, 1812

- North Sea
- NORWAY AND DENMARK
- SWEDEN
- Moscow 1812
- UNITED KINGDOM
- Friedland 1807
- RUSSIAN EMPIRE
- London
- Waterloo 1815
- ATLANTIC OCEAN
- Paris 1814
- Ulm 1805
- Austerlitz 1805
- Wagram 1809
- FRANCE
- AUSTRIAN EMPIRE
- ITALY
- Toulouse 1814
- Corsica
- Rome
- Elba
- NAPLES
- OTTOMAN EMPIRE
- Salamanca 1812
- SPAIN
- Mediterranean Sea
- Trafalgar 1812

Legend:
- French empire
- French dependency
- French ally
- □ Major battle
- ═══ Russian campaign

The years following Napoléon's defeat were no less turbulent for France. In 1848, Paris mobs removed King Louis Phillipe—another ruler who wanted total power—and established the Second Republic. His successor, Napoléon III (Napoléon Bonaparte's nephew) proved no better. He led the nation to defeat in a war with Germany in 1870, after which the French set up the Third Republic.

Hatred and distrust between France and Germany continued and contributed to the outbreak of World War I in 1914. The most destructive war in history up to that time, it pitted France, Britain, Russia, and the United States against Germany, Austria, and Turkey. Much of the fighting occurred in northern France. By the time the war ended in 1918, much of that region was in ruins and more than 1.5 million French people had been killed.

Although France emerged from the war on the winning side, it had been so devastated that recovery was difficult. Thus, it was largely unprepared when Germany, which had recovered fully from its defeat, launched World War II in 1939. Led by the Nazi dictator Adolf Hitler, German troops invaded and took control of northern France in 1940. While the Nazis occupied the country, some French joined the Resistance, a group of freedom fighters who blew up factories, armories, and bridges the Germans relied on to wage war. Nevertheless, the German occupiers used French raw materials and labor to strengthen their war effort.

General Charles de Gaulle inspecting troops during World War II

Finally came the beginning of the end of France's worst ordeal. On June 6, 1944, known as D-Day, Britain, the United States, and France's other allies landed thousands of troops on the beaches of Normandy. They swept across France, liberating the people, and then went on to capture Germany and win the war.

The Bloody D-Day Landings

On June 6, 1944, the Allies, commanded by U.S. general Dwight D. Eisenhower, began landing troops on the beaches of Normandy in northern France. Dubbed "Operation Overlord" by Eisenhower and his officers, the invasion aimed to liberate France and the rest of Europe from the Nazis. Thousands of Allied troops were killed or wounded that day as German machine guns blasted them from concrete bunkers overlooking the beaches. The fighting was especially bloody on the beach nicknamed "Omaha," an episode dramatically reenacted in Stephen Spielberg's highly acclaimed 1998 film *Saving Private Ryan*. The Allied invasion was ultimately a success, landing over a million troops in France by July 1 and leading to Nazi Germany's defeat early in 1945.

D-Day— June 6, 1944

- Allied assault formations
- Follow-up for assault corps
- Allied advance Aug.1, 1944
- Allied advance Aug. 25, 1944

France after World War II

After the conclusion of what proved to be history's most destructive war, the French established still another new government—the Fourth Republic—in 1946. It carried out many domestic economic and social reforms, including allowing women to vote. The new government also made an economic alliance with Belgium, Luxembourg, the Netherlands, West Germany, and Italy, called the European Economic Community (EEC), or Common Market. The EEC, founded in 1957, was designed to make it easier for Europeans to exchange goods and improve their economies and living conditions. The participants also hoped that it would break down their old rivalries and help them to work together in peace.

But France continued to have problems in other parts of the world. Ever since the end of World War II, French colonies in Asia and Africa had repeatedly fought the French and declared their independence. Guerrilla warfare eventually broke out between the French army and local Muslims in Algeria, a French-controlled region in North Africa. As the crisis continued, the French people became increasingly divided over how to handle it.

In 1958, with France seemingly on the brink of civil war, the French asked Charles de Gaulle, their greatest World War II hero, to step in and resolve the crisis. He said he would, on condition that he could draft a new constitution giving him almost dictatorial powers. The people agreed and the Fifth Republic was born. The new president did not disappoint his supporters. He worked out a peaceful settlement in Algeria, which became independent in 1962. His government also brought the nation increased economic stability and prosperity. De Gaulle resigned in 1969.

Since then, France has had its share of domestic political disagreements, mostly between people who want the government to exercise stricter control over private enterprise and those who do not. Yet under all of de Gaulle's successors France has remained one of the world's freest and strongest democracies. Strengthened rather than beaten by more than 2,000 years of strife and hardship, the French enter the twenty-first century with renewed energy and hope.

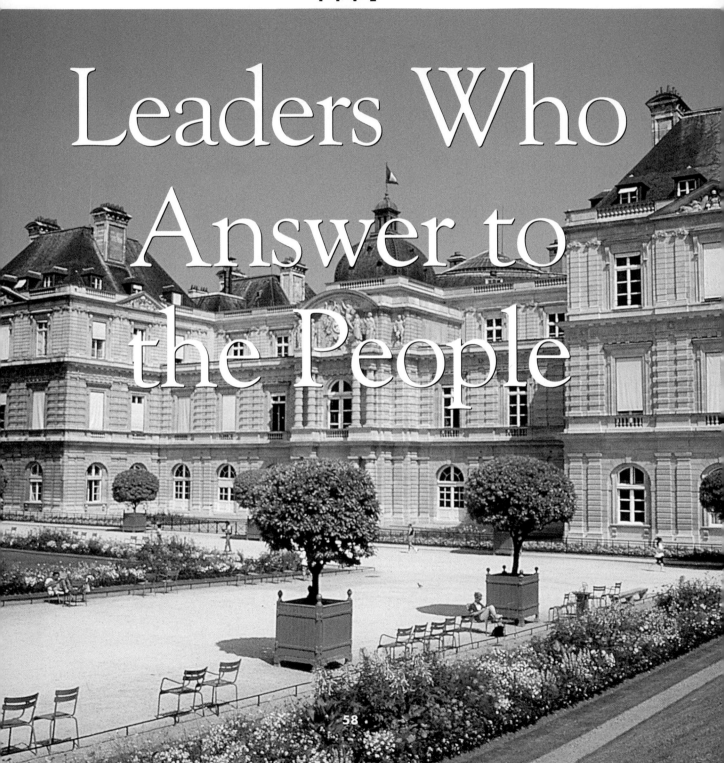

Leaders Who Answer to the People

THE DEMOCRATIC FORM OF GOVERNMENT IN FRANCE today is called the Fifth Republic. It was created in 1958 by Charles de Gaulle and his followers to replace the Fourth Republic. The Fourth Republic, which was established in 1946 after the conclusion of World War II, had proved to be inefficient and unstable. This was largely because most of the power rested in the hands of the national legislature, or parliament. By contrast, the president had very little power. Members of the parliament frequently changed their minds about the direction the country should be heading, and they just as frequently dismissed and replaced the ministers of state who were trying to run the country. In the twelve years the Fourth Republic existed, the legislature replaced the country's top leaders twenty-two times! The result was increasing political disorder and public dissatisfaction.

Eventually, it became clear to nearly all the French people that the nation needed a stronger, more stable kind of democracy. De Gaulle argued that the legislature wielded too much power and the president too little. In his view, the nation needed a stronger president who could act quickly and decisively when the legislature was bogged down in argument and indecision. A hefty majority of the French agreed with him. They voted to adopt his new constitution and have been largely content to keep it in place ever since.

Opposite: **France's Senate building, in the Luxembourg Gardens of Paris**

Charles de Gaulle

Born in 1890, Charles de Gaulle was one of France's greatest leaders, both in wartime and in peacetime. He attended military school as a boy and then fought in World War I, sustaining numerous wounds. During World War II, when the French government surrendered to the Nazis in 1940, de Gaulle and many of his followers fled to London. There he took charge of Free France, a patriotic movement intent on driving the Germans out of France. In 1943, he formed an official French government-in-exile. The following year he returned to his native land during the Allied D-Day invasion. As the nation's provisional president after the war, he helped draw up the Constitution for the Fourth Republic. But he resigned in 1946, opposed to the meager authority that constitution granted the chief executive. His instincts and foresight ultimately proved correct. In 1958, his countrymen called him out of retirement to fix the flawed constitution and lead them again. He died in 1970 at the age of eighty.

A French voter

The President and the Cabinet

Under the Fifth Republic's Constitution, the president is not only very strong, but also very independent. Although a member of one political party or another, the president does not run for office as the head of that party. The president runs for office on his or her own personal merits and answers only to the people, who have the ultimate political voice in France. French voters—men and women eighteen or older—elect their president directly every seven years.

One of the French president's most important duties is to appoint the members of his or her cabinet. The cabinet is often referred to as the "government." It is made up of various ministers of state, each in charge of a different aspect of running the country, like the Secretary of Defense or Secretary of Transportation in the United States. Along with the president, France's cabinet ministers set national policies, both domestic and foreign. They also propose most new laws. The chief minister, called the prime minister or the premier, is not as powerful as the president because the president can fire and replace the prime minister at any time.

In fact, the president of France has a number of special powers given to no one else. For example, in addition to choosing the members of the cabinet, the president can dissolve the entire elected legislature and call for new elections. Charles de Gaulle did this in October 1962 after he and the legislature failed to reach agreement on a vital issue.

The president can also call for a national referendum at any time. A national referendum is a special election in which the people vote directly on a single issue. In April 1962, for instance, de Gaulle held a referendum to decide whether Algeria should become independent from France. More than 90 percent of the French people voted yes, and the matter was settled. Thus, by appealing to the people for an immediate thumbs-up or thumbs-down on an issue, the president can avoid a long political fight with the legislature. Also, a referendum vote that supports the president's position on an issue is seen as proof that the country approves of his or her job performance.

The French Flag

France's national flag is called the "tricolor" because it features three broad stripes in three colors—blue, white, and red. Red and blue were long the symbolic colors of Paris, and white was the color most often used by French royalty. During the early stages of the French Revolution, the new republican government adopted a flag combining the three colors. The red and blue stripes enclose the white, in a sense suggesting the people's control of the monarchy and therefore their freedom. Except for a short period in the early 1800s, the tricolor has been France's flag ever since.

In addition, in an extreme emergency the president can assume nearly dictatorial powers for a temporary period. What is more, he or she cannot be impeached, or removed from office, except on a charge of "high treason"—such as betraying the nation to a foreign enemy. In other words, the chief executive cannot be fired for such offenses as misusing public funds or lying to the people. Some French people worry that the president's powers are too great. They fear that someday a person may use these powers to make himself or herself a dictator. So far, however, no one has abused the position in this manner, so most voters see no compelling reason to change the system.

Checks and Balances

François Mitterrand campaigning

Most French people do not worry about their president becoming a dictator because their system is a democracy in which power is ultimately in the hands of the voters. An example of how the people can act to check and balance the system occurred in 1986. The president, François Mitterrand, belonged to the left-wing Socialist Party. Because he had been elected in 1981, his seven-year term would not be over until 1988. But in the 1986 legislative elections, the voters elected a majority of right-wing

Paris: Did You Know This?

Paris lies on the Seine River about 90 miles (145 km) southeast of the river's mouth on the English Channel. The Hôtel de Ville (City Hall) is shown above.

Population: 2,175,200 (Paris Region: 10,650,000)

Founded: about 250 B.C. by Celtic tribesmen as a fishing village

Average Daily Temperature: 75°F (24°C) in July; 43°F (6°C) in January

Average Annual Rainfall: 23 inches (58 cm)

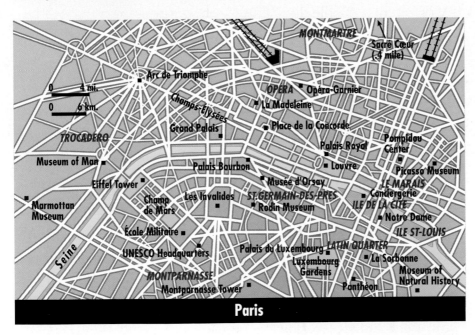

NATIONAL GOVERNMENT OF FRANCE

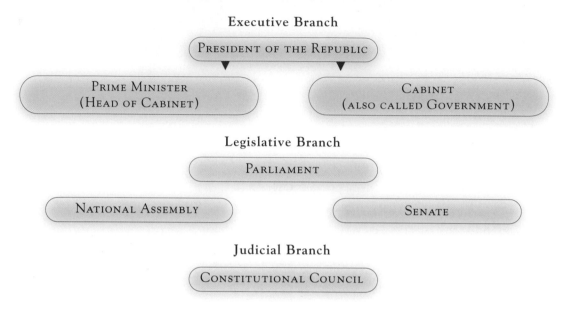

Executive Branch

PRESIDENT OF THE REPUBLIC

PRIME MINISTER
(HEAD OF CABINET)

CABINET
(ALSO CALLED GOVERNMENT)

Legislative Branch

PARLIAMENT

NATIONAL ASSEMBLY

SENATE

Judicial Branch

CONSTITUTIONAL COUNCIL

politicians to the legislature. This marked the first time in the history of the Fifth Republic that the majority in the parliament belonged to a different party than the president.

Mitterrand could have dissolved the legislature and called for a new election in which left-wing candidates might be chosen. But this would have made him seem biased in favor of a single party rather than impartial, as the president is supposed to be. He knew that the French people would have seen such a move as an abuse of power. To be impartial—and thereby maintain his popularity—Mitterrand appointed a right-wing prime minister, Jacques Chirac. The end result was a left-wing president who checked and balanced a right-wing legislature and prime minister, and vice-versa. The people's will largely prevailed.

The National Legislature

The French national legislature, or parliament, consists of two houses, the National Assembly and the Senate. The stronger and politically more important of the two, the National Assembly, has 577 members who are elected directly by the people and serve for five years. They, like their counterparts in the U.S. Congress, propose new legislation. In France, however, more than 90 percent of such bills are formulated by the cabinet ministers. That means that the National Assembly spends most of its time debating, amending, and voting on the bills the government sends it.

The interior of France's National Assembly building

The other legislative house, the Senate, has 321 members who serve nine-year terms. They are elected indirectly, rather than directly by the people. The people elect various national, regional, and city officials and these officials, called Great Electors, hold special meetings in which they choose the members of the Senate. Like the National Assembly, the Senate debates and amends legislation. But the Senate wields less power than the National Assembly, which can pass bills without the Senate's approval. The Senate has one unique power, though. The nation has no elected vice president, and if the president resigns or dies in office, the leader of the Senate becomes acting president until new elections can be held.

France has no supreme court as the United States has. So a French citizen on trial cannot appeal to a higher court on the grounds that the law he or she is accused of is unconstitutional. Instead, a body called the Constitutional Council examines controversial laws *before* they are approved by the legislature. The Council has nine members who serve nine-year terms. Three are appointed by the president, three by the head of the National Assembly, and three by the head of the Senate. The Council also possesses the power to nullify an election and call for a new one if it finds evidence of fraud.

Regional and Local Government

In addition to its national government, France has regional governments similar in some ways to those of U.S. states. As the United States is divided into fifty states, France is divided into ninety-six departments. Each department has a general council

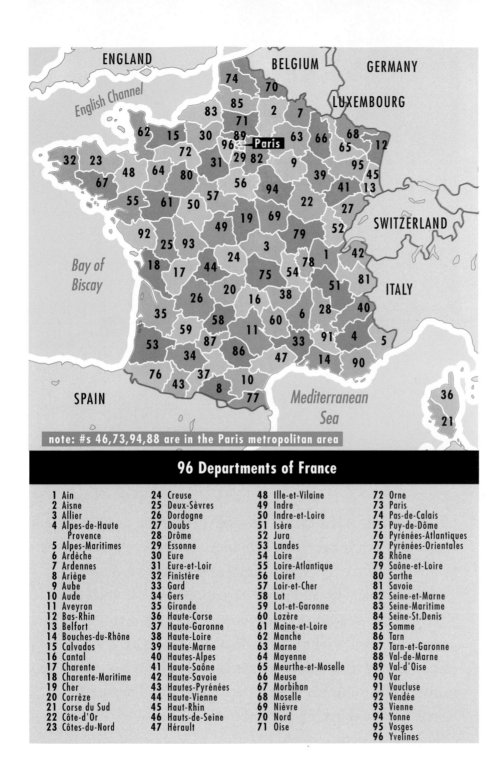

96 Departments of France

note: #s 46,73,94,88 are in the Paris metropolitan area

1 Ain	24 Creuse	48 Ille-et-Vilaine	72 Orne
2 Aisne	25 Deux-Sèvres	49 Indre	73 Paris
3 Allier	26 Dordogne	50 Indre-et-Loire	74 Pas-de-Calais
4 Alpes-de-Haute Provence	27 Doubs	51 Isère	75 Puy-de-Dôme
	28 Drôme	52 Jura	76 Pyrénées-Atlantiques
5 Alpes-Maritimes	29 Essonne	53 Landes	77 Pyrénées-Orientales
6 Ardèche	30 Eure	54 Loire	78 Rhône
7 Ardennes	31 Eure-et-Loir	55 Loire-Atlantique	79 Saône-et-Loire
8 Ariège	32 Finistère	56 Loiret	80 Sarthe
9 Aube	33 Gard	57 Loir-et-Cher	81 Savoie
10 Aude	34 Gers	58 Lot	82 Seine-et-Marne
11 Aveyron	35 Gironde	59 Lot-et-Garonne	83 Seine-Maritime
12 Bas-Rhin	36 Haute-Corse	60 Lozère	84 Seine-St.Denis
13 Belfort	37 Haute-Garonne	61 Maine-et-Loire	85 Somme
14 Bouches-du-Rhône	38 Haute-Loire	62 Manche	86 Tarn
15 Calvados	39 Haute-Marne	63 Marne	87 Tarn-et-Garonne
16 Cantal	40 Hautes-Alpes	64 Mayenne	88 Val-de-Marne
17 Charente	41 Haute-Saône	65 Meurthe-et-Moselle	89 Val-d'Oise
18 Charente-Maritime	42 Haute-Savoie	66 Meuse	90 Var
19 Cher	43 Hautes-Pyrénées	67 Morbihan	91 Vaucluse
20 Corrèze	44 Haute-Vienne	68 Moselle	92 Vendée
21 Corse du Sud	45 Haut-Rhin	69 Nièvre	93 Vienne
22 Côte-d'Or	46 Hauts-de-Seine	70 Nord	94 Yonne
23 Côtes-du-Nord	47 Hérault	71 Oise	95 Vosges
			96 Yvelines

A regional government building in Montpellier

of officials elected by the people and a governor, called a prefect, appointed by the president's cabinet. Together, the prefect and general council oversee and direct a department's affairs.

On the local level, France has about 38,000 town and city governments known as communes. The people living in each commune elect a council of officials, and these officials then elect a mayor from their own ranks. Paris, France's capital city, is unusual in that it is both a department and a commune. So it operates under both a regional government, headed by a commissioner, and a local one, headed by a mayor.

President Jacques Chirac

Jacques Chirac (1932–) is the leader of France's conservative Republic or Gaullist party. Elected to France's National Assembly in 1967, he held several cabinet posts before becoming prime minister for the first time in 1974. Later, he served as mayor of Paris and in 1981 made an unsuccessful bid for the presidency. In 1986, Chirac served a second term as prime minister but then lost another bid for the presidency two years later. In his third try for France's top political office, in 1995, he finally tasted victory.

CONFÉRENCE DE PAIX SUR L'EX-YOUGOSLAVIE
PARIS

France's National Anthem

Composed by a French soldier in 1792 during the Revolution, the French national anthem, *The Marseillaise*, is widely considered to be the world's most stirring national song. Here is an English translation of some of its many verses:

Arise children of the fatherland, the day of glory has arrived.
Against us tyranny's bloody standard is raised.
Listen to the sounds in the fields, the howling of these fearsome soldiers.
They are coming into our midst to cut the throats of your sons and wives.
To arms citizens! Form your battalions!
March, march! Let impure blood water our fields!
Drive on sacred patriotism. Support our avenging arms.
Liberty, cherished liberty, join the struggle with your defenders.
Under our flags, let victory hurry to your manly tone,
So that in death your enemies see your triumph and our glory!

A Diversified Economy

FRANCE HAS HAD ONE OF THE WORLD'S LEADING ECONOMIES for a very long time. The French countryside early showed its vast agricultural potential when, as Gaul, it supplied the Roman Empire with most of the crops and livestock it needed. Later, mining and manufacturing developed in France, supplementing agriculture, and by the early 1700s, France was one of the world's wealthiest nations. Like Britain, the United States, and some other countries, France began industrializing in the late 1700s and early 1800s. But French industrial output soon lagged behind that of other developed countries and agriculture long remained France's chief economic base.

In the years following World War II, however, the French economy greatly increased in both size and diversity. Agriculture remained important, but increasing numbers of people gave up farming for steadier, better-paying work in factories and businesses. In 1939, just prior to the outbreak of World War II, about 35 percent of French workers made their living by farming, the highest proportion in Europe. By 1983 that figure had fallen to 8 percent and is still decreasing. In the same year, by contrast, industrial and manufacturing jobs employed almost 25 percent of France's labor force.

This shift in the country's economic base vastly increased France's already considerable economic output, making it a major exporting nation. In the postwar years, both the French government and private investors put much time, effort, and

Opposite: **Sunflowers are a cash crop grown in France for sale to other countries.**

Citroën bodies are ready to take their place on the assembly line

French textiles are sold around the world.

money into expanding industries, such as coal, natural gas, electricity, chemicals, and textiles. Production of cars, trucks, ships, and airplanes also increased significantly. The French shipped these products all over the world, and by 1980 France was the world's fifth-largest exporter of goods. By the late 1990s, it was the fourth-largest, with overall exports worth $285 billion.

Valuable Economic Partnerships

Of these substantial exports, 65 percent, or about two-thirds, goes to France's European trade partners. The development of economic partnerships with its neighbors has provided

Money Facts

France's main unit of currency is the *franc*. It is divided into 100 smaller units called *centimes*. Paper money comes in notes worth 500, 200, 100, 50, and 20 francs. Coins are worth 10, 5, 2, and 1 franc, and there are also coins worth 1/2 franc and 20, 10, and 5 centimes. In 1999, a 100-franc bill was worth about U.S.$16. The woman whose likeness appears on the backs of French coins is Liberté, who represents freedom.

France, like most other member nations of the European Union, has begun the process of converting to the *Euro*, the new European currency. In 2002, the Euro will replace the franc.

France with ready, reliable markets for its goods and has helped the nation to maintain a prosperous and steadily growing economy. The first such partnership formed in 1957 when

Unloading containers from a ship in Port Saint-Louis du Rhône, Provence

The European Union

the French joined in creating the six-member European Economic Community (EEC), or Common Market. By 1995, the successful EEC had become the even more successful European Union (EU), with fifteen member countries.

Because there are no trade barriers between these countries, it costs the French less to deal with them than with other nations. And France's neighbors clearly like its products. In 1995, France exported $13 billion more in goods to EU members than it imported from them. This difference between exports and imports, called a trade surplus, has helped keep the French economy healthy.

French Agriculture

Today there are about 730,000 farms and 910,000 farmworkers in France, far fewer than before World War II. Yet the country did not, as might be expected, undergo a corresponding reduction in crop and livestock production. In fact, more advanced farming tools and methods, along with modern fertilizers and insect sprays, have actually increased the nation's agricultural output. In the late 1990s, France was the world's second-largest exporter of farm products.

French agriculture underwent other major changes besides modernization in the second half of the twentieth century. First, most farms increased in size. Many traditional family farms, averaging 8 to 10 acres (3 to 4 ha), bought out their neighbors' lands or combined into much larger farming cooperatives. This trend, in which farming became a big, high-powered business, occurred mainly because of the establishment of the EEC. The Common Market's reduced trade barriers allowed French farmers to export much larger quantities of grain, milk, butter, beef, and other foodstuffs than ever before. Today, about 115,800 square miles (299,920 sq km) of France, slightly more than half the country's area, is used for agricultural production.

Spraying crops from a helicopter

Wine grapes being harvested in Languedoc

Many French farmers also began growing new, valuable cash crops that were popular in foreign countries. Among these are maize (a sweet corn), sunflowers, and other crops used in making cooking oils. Meanwhile traditional French crops and products, such as wheat, barley, sugar beets, beef, poultry, milk, and wine remain as important as ever. France ranks first in the EU in the production of sugar beets and beef and second in the world in making wine.

What France Grows, Makes, and Mines

Agriculture

Wheat	35,000,000 metric tons
Sugar beets	30,000,000 metric tons
Corn (maize)	14,000,000 metric tons

Manufacturing

Steel	18,000,000 metric tons
Cars	3,600,000 units
Chemicals, rubber, plastics	U.S.$70,000,000,000 worth

Mining

Natural gas	10,000,000 cubic meters
Coals	9,000,000 metric tons
Crude petroleum	3,000,000 metric tons

Industry and Manufacturing in France

France's industries, like its general economy, are highly diversified. They mine important raw materials, including coal,

Potash production in Alsace

iron, bauxite, potash, petroleum, and natural gas. They also manufacture these materials into usable products. For example, coal and petroleum are used to produce electricity in France (although the French rely more heavily on nuclear power plants for their electrical needs). Potash is a major component of chemicals and fertilizers, of which France is

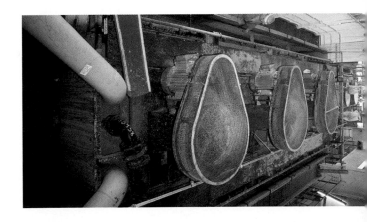

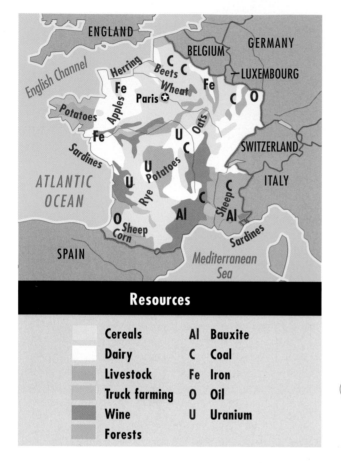

Resources

	Cereals	Al	Bauxite
	Dairy	C	Coal
	Livestock	Fe	Iron
	Truck farming	O	Oil
	Wine	U	Uranium
	Forests		

the world's fourth-largest exporter. And French factories turn bauxite, a mineral, into aluminum.

Other factories use the aluminum along with steel and other products to make cars and other vehicles and machines. The French were pioneers in automotive manufacturing almost a century ago, and now France has the fourth-largest automobile industry in the world, turning out some 3,600,000 cars each year. France also produces over $23 billion worth of ships, aircraft, and trains per year.

The Nation's Industrial Areas

One of France's main industrial zones is in the northern reaches of the Massif Central. The plateau used to be rich in minerals, including coal, copper, lead, and iron, but years of mining have significantly depleted the known deposits. Coal mining in the area has been particularly hard-hit, declining by

Rich and Poor

France has one of the strongest economies and highest standards of living in Europe. Yet there is a wider gap between rich and poor people in France than in most other European nations. The top 1 percent of the French own 20 percent of the country's private wealth, while the bottom 10 percent of the people possess only 0.1 percent. The average manager of a French business makes seven times as much money as the unskilled workers he or she supervises.

50 percent since the 1950s. But some of the plateau's industrial towns, most notably Clermont-Ferrand and Saint-Étienne, are still prosperous. Clermont-Ferrand not only produces many heavy steel goods, such as airplane engines and railroad equipment, but also has one of the world's largest tire factories.

Despite decreased coal mining in the Massif Central, France still produces a lot of coal, mostly in two other important industrial areas. One is in the far north, near Lille, on the Belgian border. The other is in the northeast, near Metz. Natural-gas production is centered mainly at Pau and Lacq, in the Pyrenees foothills in southern France. When discovered in 1951, the gas deposits at Lacq were the second-largest in Europe, but constant production has caused them to shrink considerably since that time. Another major French industrial zone lies in the Paris region, where thousands of factories turn out clothing, luxury articles, cars, engineering equipment, and food products.

Tourism

France's beautiful landscapes and rich culture attract more than 60 million foreign tourists each year. Among the chief attractions are shopping and restaurants, world-class museums, Alpine ski resorts, the beaches on the Mediterranean coast, and world-famous vineyards and wineries. More than a million French people work in the tourist industry, which brings billions of dollars a year into the country, making it one of the most important sectors of France's economy. The Centre Pompidou, a museum of modern art in Paris named after President Georges Pompidou, is shown at left.

The People's Origins and Language

Mᴏʀᴇ ᴛʜᴀɴ 58 ᴍɪʟʟɪᴏɴ ᴘᴇᴏᴘʟᴇ ʟɪᴠᴇ ɪɴ Fʀᴀɴᴄᴇ ᴛᴏᴅᴀʏ. Generally, the areas with the most industry, business activity, and/or tourism have the largest and fastest-growing populations. These include the mining and industrial regions of the north and northeast, the Lyon region in the Rhône-Saône Corridor, the Côte d'Azur in the southeast, and, especially, the Paris region. By contrast, areas with no industry or with poor soils that cannot support agriculture are sparsely populated.

This distribution of people within the country was a result of major population shifts that occurred mainly in the years after World War II. In 1850, France had about 36 million people, and the number of people born each year was increasing.

Opposite: **Provençal shepherds moving their flocks**

Paris in the early twentieth century, including the Arc de Triomphe and the Champs-Élysées

But in the late 1800s and early 1900s, France's birthrate dropped significantly and the country began to experience slower population growth than other European nations. Large numbers of the French still lived on farms and in rural areas, and most cities remained small by European standards. The birthrate increased sharply after World War II, however, when France rapidly industrialized. And many people moved from rural areas into the cities and industrial regions.

Rapid Urbanization and Rural Depopulation

Because cities are referred to as urban areas, the growth of cities is called urbanization. The most marked example of post-

A deserted farmhouse in the Massif Central

war urbanization in France took place in the Paris region (metropolitan Paris)—the city and its surrounding suburbs and industrial centers. In 1911, the population of the Paris region was just over 5 million. By the early 1990s, that number had almost doubled to more than 10 million, nearly one-sixth of France's total population. About one-fifth of this total, a little over 2 million people, now live in the city's downtown sector, but many people live in the suburbs and commute to work in the city each day. Similar, though smaller, examples of rapid urbanization and metropolitan growth occurred in other parts of France.

One major effect of all of this urban growth was a corresponding drop in the number of people in the countryside. In other words, so many people moved into the cities that the populations of many rural towns and villages became very small. Some villages and areas, mostly in the Pyrenees and the Massif Central, were actually deserted. This trend slowed somewhat in the 1980s and 1990s, partly because some city dwellers began buying and restoring old houses in the abandoned areas to use as vacation or retirement homes.

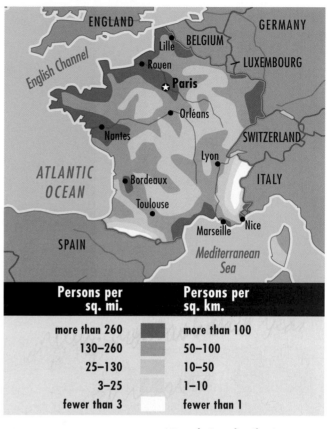

Persons per sq. mi.		Persons per sq. km.
more than 260		more than 100
130–260		50–100
25–130		10–50
3–25		1–10
fewer than 3		fewer than 1

Population distribution in France

Populations of France's Largest Cities (downtown sectors; 1990 census)	
Paris	2,175,200
Marseille	807,726
Lyon	422,444
Toulouse	365,933
Nice	345,674
Strasbourg	255,937

Teenage girls exchange a typical greeting.

Taking a break from traffic

Origins of France's Natives and Immigrants

Today, as in the past, most French people were born in France. However, because many outside groups settled permanently and intermarried in the country's long history, the native French have a mixed ancestry. That ancestry includes Celtic, Latin (Roman), German, Scandinavian (Viking), and other groups. In fact, the intermixing of these groups has been going on for so long that today it is difficult to figure out an average French person's ethnic origins.

The origins of one small group of natives, the Basques, are particularly hard to trace. The Basques have lived in the sheltered valleys and hillsides of the western Pyrenees Mountains in southern France and northern Spain for more than 2,000 years. While the French call them Basques, and the Spanish call them *vascos*, they refer to themselves as the *Euskaldunak*. No one knows their origins because their language is unrelated to any European tongue. From their mountain strongholds, these ancient and mysterious people managed to fight off Roman, German, Muslim, and other invaders over the centuries. They finally lost their independence to the French after the 1789 Revolution. Even so, the Basques stubbornly held onto their language and customs. Today there are about 90,000 Basque speakers in France, and several thousand others also identify themselves as Basques.

By contrast, the origins of the foreign immigrants who entered France in the twentieth century are well known. In the postwar years, when French industry was rapidly expanding, the creation of new factory jobs attracted many foreign workers. Among these were immigrants from Spain, Portugal, Poland, Italy, and France's former colonies in North Africa and Southeast Asia. The quickly growing French automobile industry particularly came to depend on these foreign workers, who were often willing to work for low wages.

Basque men

French schoolchildren

An Algerian immigrant

North Africans are not always accepted in France as easily as other immigrants.

The French Muslims

The largest single group of immigrants to France in these years was Muslims who came mostly from the former French colony of Algeria. Algerians and other people of North African origin now make up about 80 percent of the total of over 5 million immigrants living in France. And North Africans make up more than 30 percent of the overall immigrant workforce, which totals nearly 2 million.

Most of France's immigrants, especially those of European ancestry, have found the native-born French to be friendly and accepting. The North Africans have had a more difficult time assimilating, however. This is partly because of tensions stemming from racial and cultural differences. The North Africans are darker-skinned than most French, and most are Muslims, who practice the faith of Islam, rather than Christianity, the country's main religion. Also, many native-born French have accused North Africans, as well as other immigrants, of taking jobs from French people. By the mid-1990s, France had an unemployment rate of nearly 12 percent, more than twice that of the United States.

In the 1980s, this resentment led to the formation of a right-wing political party, the National Front Party, formed with the aim of stopping Muslim immigration. Using the racist slogan "France for the French," the party's leader managed to win more than 14 percent of the vote in the 1988 elections. Since that time the National Front Party has lost some ground, but racial tensions persist. Some of the Beurs—children born in France of Muslim immigrant parents—still experience hatred and racial attacks even though they are French speaking and French-educated.

France's Immigrant Workforce (early 1990s, est.)	
Portuguese	29%
Algerian	16%
Moroccan	12%
Spanish	7%
Italian	6%
Tunisian	4%
All others	26%

Language

It would seem logical that, with people from so many foreign lands living in France, the country would have many different languages. But this is not the case. First, foreign immigrants make up only about 10 percent of the population. Also, most of these people speak French in addition to their native tongue. So French remains the nation's main language.

In fact, most French people are very proud of their language. French is called a Romance language (along with Italian, Spanish, and some others) because it developed from Latin, the language of the Romans. (The term *Romance* comes from the Latin phrase *romanica loqui*, meaning "to speak in Roman fashion.")

The French have long recognized that spoken words change faster than written ones and that the influx of foreign words and phrases can steadily change a language. In 1635, to protect their native tongue from such changes, they established the *Académie française*, or French Academy. It consists of

Signs in French surround this Paris métro station.

French Pronunciation Key

This chart shows the French letter sounds that differ the most from English letter sounds.

Letter(s)	Pronounce as	Example	Pronunciation
é	ay	*enchanté*	on-shon-TAY
u	No English equivalent. Round the lips as if to pronounce the letter o, then say ee.		
ç	s	*garçon*	gar-SOH (The letter *n* at the end of a word is usually silent.)
oi	wah	*soir*	sWAH
gn	nyuh	*campagne*	kam-PAHN-yuh
h	Never pronounced, so:		
th	t	*théâtre*	tay-AH-tr (the final tr is trilled rather than pronounced)

forty scholars who are appointed for life. They keep track of new words entering the language, decide which words should be allowed in the official dictionary, and set standards of usage.

The members of the Academy, along with many other French citizens, became alarmed in the twentieth century as thousands of English words and phrases became common in spoken French. This mixture of the two languages came to be called *franglais*. To discourage the use of franglais, the French legislature passed a law in 1994 making it compulsory to use standard French in all public notices and advertisements.

Still, many people in France continue to deviate from standard French in ordinary conversation. Several dialects of French are spoken around the country. In the northeastern Alsace and Lorraine regions, for example, people use a dialect that mixes French and German. In Brittany, in the northwest, the dialect is Breton, a mixture of French and English. And in southeastern France, the site of Rome's original Gallic province, the most common dialect is Provençal, which retains many Latin influences.

Common French Words and Phrases

Adieu or Au revoir.	Good-bye.
Bonjour.	Hello *or* Good day.
Comment ça va?	How are you?
De rien.	You're welcome.
Pourquoi?	Why?
Excusez-moi.	Excuse me.
Je m'appelle . . .	My name is . . .
Merci.	Thank-you.
non	no
oui	yes
pardon	sorry
Parlez-vous anglais?	Do you speak English?
Quelle heure est-il?	What time is it?
s'il vous plaît	please

French Phrases Used in English

avant-garde	ahead of its time, especially in the arts
Bon appétit!	Enjoy your meal!
carte blanche	given complete power or permission
C'est la vie.	That's life.
crème de la crème	the best
déjà vu	the feeling you have seen something before
esprit de corps	group spirit
faux pas	a mistake
laissez-faire	leave alone
par excellence	to the highest degree
raison d'être	a reason for existing
tour de force	an outstanding feat

The Elder Daughter of the Church

I N 1980, POPE JOHN PAUL II, SPIRITUAL LEADER OF THE world's Roman Catholics, visited France. Addressing a crowd of over 500,000 people, he asked them, "France, what have you done with your baptism?" He was referring to the baptism of Clovis, the Frankish chief, in the year 496. The French and other Europeans later viewed Clovis's conversion as the beginning of Christianity's long and proud tradition as France's official religion. It remained that way until 1905, when the government of the Third Republic passed laws separating church and state. In fact, the French were such devout Christians for so many centuries that their nation came to be called *la fille aînée de l'église*, "the elder daughter of the church."

Cathedrals and Saints

All through medieval times and well into early modern times, the Roman Catholic Church, its teachings, and its clergy remained guiding forces in everyday French life. Almost everyone, rich or poor, worshiped regularly, and they closely observed religious customs and ceremonies such as baptism, holy communion, and Lent. The

A Visit to the Cathedral of Notre Dame

Paris's Cathedral of Notre Dame is the city's most enduring landmark and one of Europe's greatest surviving examples of Gothic architecture. Located on the Île de la Cité, an island in the Seine River, it was begun in 1163 and completed in 1345. The best time to visit the cathedral's interior is in the early morning. Soft, multicolored shafts of light from the beautiful stained-glass windows illuminate parts of the vast and otherwise dimly lit nave, or central hall. To reach the tops of the famous towers, you must climb 387 steps. But the effort is rewarded with a magnificent view of the city. The south tower houses the cathedral's great bell, the one supposedly tolled by Quasimodo, the fictional title character in Victor Hugo's *Hunchback of Notre Dame*.

Saint Vincent de Paul

Born into a French peasant family in 1581, Vincent de Paul became the patron saint of charitable works and one of France's best-remembered religious figures. As a young man he joined the priesthood and dedicated his life to helping the poor. He founded several charitable organizations, as well as seminaries to train young men to be priests. He died in 1660 and the Catholic Church made him a saint in 1737. The St. Vincent de Paul Society still conducts charitable activities in his honor.

people also expressed their fervent devotion to God by erecting magnificent churches and cathedrals. Among the finest and most famous are the Cathedral of Notre Dame in Paris, completed in 1345, and its namesake at Chartres, about 55 miles (88 km) southwest of Paris, finished in 1220. The Chartres Cathedral has many windows in which inspiring religious scenes are depicted using some of the finest stained glass ever crafted in Europe.

France has also produced more than its share of religious martyrs and saints. Perhaps the most familiar of these figures outside France is Joan of Arc, who was burned at the stake in 1431 on a trumped-up charge of witchcraft. The Catholic Church made her a saint in 1920. Another important French religious figure who later became a saint was Francis de Sales (1567–1622). He is best known for his writings, especially his *Introduction to a Devout Life*, intended to help people become more spiritual. In 1923, the Catholic Church proclaimed him the patron saint of all Catholic writers. Other memorable French religious figures were Saint Vincent de Paul (born in 1581), noted for his charitable work, and Saint Bernadette (born in 1844), who claimed she had personal contact with the Virgin Mary.

Saint Bernadette and the Miracle of Lourdes

Bernadette Soubirous (1844–1879) was a Frenchwoman who became known world-wide for her religious visions. She claimed that in 1858, when she was fourteen, the Virgin Mary visited her eighteen times in a cave near Lourdes in southern France. Many people called her visions a miracle and came to believe that the waters of a nearby spring had healing properties. Bernadette became a saint in 1933. Today, up to 5 million people visit the cave at Lourdes every year, many of them hoping that miracles will heal their illnesses.

Catholics versus Protestants

Because the Catholic faith was so firmly entrenched in France, the nation turned into a religious battleground when church reformers came along in the sixteenth century. The religious makeup of the country in later times, including the present, was largely determined by this conflict. The so-called Reformation began in the mid-1500s when a number of European clergymen tried to rid the Catholic Church of what they saw as corrupt practices. One of these men was a French religious leader named John Calvin. The reformers' efforts met with fierce opposition. The Church was soon divided between the Catholics, who still followed the pope in Rome, and the Protestants, who no longer recognized the pope's authority.

In France, Calvin's Protestant followers were called Huguenots. Between 1562 and 1598, the Huguenots and Catholics engaged in several rounds of bloody warfare.

Persecution of the Huguenots in the 1600s

The bloodiest battle of all was the Saint Bartholomew's Day Massacre, on August 24, 1572. On that day, the Catholics butchered untold thousands of Huguenots all over France.

The fighting finally ended in 1598, after King Henry IV, a Protestant, converted to Catholicism. But anti-Protestant persecutions continued in the 1600s, causing over 250,000 French Protestants to flee to England, the Netherlands, Germany, Switzerland, and other lands. These events explain why Protestants, once quite numerous in France, make up only about 2 percent of the population today.

John Calvin

Frenchman Jean (John) Calvin (1509–1564) was one of the principal leaders of the Reformation, the sixteenth-century religious movement that separated Protestant churches from the Catholic Church. After studying in Paris as a young man, Calvin became involved in efforts to reform the Christian Church. Over time, he developed a comprehensive set of religious ideas and rules, which he set down in his *Institutes of the Christian Religion* (1536). Calvin eventually helped establish the Presbyterian movement, in which church members who are not priests play important leadership roles. His beliefs and writings influenced millions of people in Europe and other parts of the world.

Jews and Muslims

The Protestants were not the only religious minority in France to feel the sting of intolerance and persecution. Jews have made up a small but productive portion of France's population since medieval times. For many centuries, French Jews, like their brethren in other parts of Europe, were not allowed to own property or become citizens. They were also forced to live apart from Christians. In addition, Jews were frequently arrested, killed, or banished for crimes they did not commit. In 1306, for instance, almost all of France's Jews were forced to leave the country because of such false rumors.

After the French Revolution, which promoted the ideal of brotherhood, treatment of French Jews improved greatly and Jews were granted full civil rights. But some anti-Jewish prejudices remained. They resurfaced in the 1890s when a French Jew, army officer Alfred Dreyfus, was falsely accused of betraying the country.

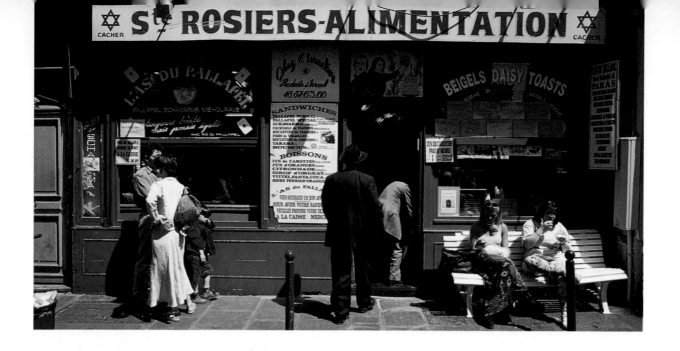

Persecution of French Jews continued in the twentieth century. As many as 75,000 of them suffered and died in Nazi prison camps, sent there during World War II with the cooperation of French officials who were working with the Germans. Fortunately, however, Jewish life in France improved again after the war. Today Jews number over half

A delicatessen in the Jewish quarter of Paris

Religious Prejudice: The Dreyfus Affair

Over the years, France has seen its share of religious hatred, including some directed at its Jewish citizens. The most famous example was the case of Alfred Dreyfus (right), a French army officer. In 1894, largely because he happened to be Jewish, he was falsely accused of passing information to a German agent. A court-martial found him guilty and sent him to prison. Led by the popular French writer Émile Zola, many influential French people fought to get the case reopened. They eventually proved that the evidence against Dreyfus had been forged, and in 1906 a civilian court cleared him.

Children in front of a storefront mosque in Dunkerque

a million, about 1 percent of the country's population, the highest proportion living in any western European nation.

The twentieth century also witnessed distrust and intolerance of another French religious minority—the Muslims. When large numbers of Muslims from Algeria and Morocco entered France in the 1960s, they fast became the largest such

A large mosque in Paris

Religions of France

Roman Catholic	82%
Muslim	7%
Protestant	2%
Jewish	1%
Other (Eastern faiths, atheists, etc.)	8%

minority in the country. Like French Jews and Protestants before them, many French Muslims felt—and still feel—that French Christians resented and discriminated against them. As proof, they cited the popularity in the 1980s and 1990s of the National Front Party, whose members often criticized Muslim religious practices for being "un-French."

Whatever the degree of anti-Muslim feelings in France, the Muslims are in the country to stay. They attend schools, own property, and run businesses, just as other French people do. And they have built over 900 mosques—Muslim places of worship—in France, a little over a quarter of them in and around Paris.

Church Attendance

Because Muslims, Protestants, and Jews are still relatively small minorities in France, Catholicism remains France's major religion. At least this is how it appears on the surface. Polls and studies show that about 80 percent of the French identify themselves as Catholics. Yet the same polls and studies reveal that only about half of France's Catholics actually attend church. And most of those who do go to church attend only on special occasions such as births, marriages, and funerals. Only about 8 percent of French Catholics attend church services every week. By contrast, about 50 percent of the Catholics in the United States are weekly churchgoers.

The reasons for this marked decline in what was once the most devout religious community in Europe are unclear. Some French people blame a decrease in moral values and a rise in "greed" and "selfishness" caused by an increasing desire for material goods. Others say that many French have been turned off by rigid church rules, especially regarding sexual matters. Most French, including most Catholics, feel that church leaders have no business telling them how to conduct their personal and family matters. Another reason that French churches are frequently empty is that many French Catholics choose to worship at home. Typically they meet in groups for prayer and discussion, often with no priest present.

Whatever the causes of declining church attendance and influence, some of the more devout French Catholics are worried. They fear that French Catholicism is becoming more a social tradition and less an actual belief system. In an effort to increase church attendance, in 1992 a group of Paris Catholics launched a series of TV spots urging people to celebrate Easter. This plan seemed to backfire, however. Large numbers of the French criticized the ads, saying that they reduced religion to a mere product.

French (Catholic) Religious Holidays and Observances

L'Epiphanie (Epiphany)	January 6
Le Carnaval (Carnival)	Last day before Lent
La Chandeleur (Feast of the Virgin)	February 2
Pâques (Easter)	Varies
L'Ascension (Ascension)	Forty days after Easter
La Pentecôte (Pentecost)	Fifty days after Easter
L'Assomption (Assumption)	August 15
La Toussaint (All Saints' Day)	November 1
Noël (Christmas)	December 25

CHAPTER NINE

The Finer Things in Life

FRENCH CULTURE, INCLUDING PAINTING, SCULPTURE, ARCHI-
tecture, music, literature, and film, is world renowned. In fact,
after Greece and Italy, France has influenced and helped to
shape the arts and letters of Western (European-based) society
more than any other nation. For example, cathedrals in the
Gothic style, which originated in
northern France, can be found all
over Europe. And artists of every
nationality continue to turn out
paintings in the impressionist style
pioneered by nineteenth-century
French artists.

Because of France's long history of innovating and perfecting
the creative arts, its people have
come to love and support cultural
endeavors of all kinds. They
understand the need for creative
people to express themselves,
even if it means doing without
creature comforts. The familiar
stereotype of the young, starving
artist is based on real artists of the
past who lived in run-down, one-
room Paris apartments.

Opposite: **The Louvre in
Paris is the largest museum
in the world.**

**The cathedral of Reims is
built in the Gothic style.**

The World's Largest Museum

The Louvre, located on the banks of the Seine River in the heart of Paris, is the largest—and many say the most beautiful—art museum in the world. It was originally built as a fortress in the thirteenth century. Later, many French monarchs used it as a palace, expanding it little by little. After the French Revolution, it became a museum. Among the Louvre's thousands of fabulous attractions are ancient Egyptian, Greek, and Roman artifacts, and paintings and sculptures by European masters. The museum's main attraction by far, however, is Leonardo da Vinci's famous painting, the *Mona Lisa*, which the French call *La Joconde*.

Most French enjoy going to museums, and France has some of the finest in the world, including the marvelous Louvre, in Paris. They also like to read and to attend concerts and films. Such cultural endeavors, the French will tell you, are "the finer things," which give life meaning, value, and pleasure. Most French people take pride in their appreciation of the arts and consider a person who cares nothing for art and culture to be uncivilized.

Detail of a stained-glass window in Chartres

Architecture

The first French architectural style to spread throughout Europe was the Gothic. Gothic cathedrals have huge naves, or central halls, with very high ceilings and many stained-glass windows. To keep these large halls from collapsing, French architects developed massive external supports called flying buttresses. Gothic cathedrals also

The towers of some Gothic cathedrals are decorated with gargoyles and other elaborate sculptures.

feature dizzyingly tall towers decorated with elaborate sculptures, including grotesque figures called gargoyles. The first Gothic cathedrals were built in the mid-1100s in northern France. The largest and most famous stand in Paris, Chartres, Amiens, Rouen, and Reims.

Many magnificent palaces and other buildings were erected in France in the sixteenth and seventeenth centuries. Their design was strongly influenced by Italian styles that had developed in the 1400s. The marriage of Italian and French styles reached its climax in the late 1600s in huge and splendid additions to the Louvre and the construction of the luxurious Palace of Versailles.

Painting and Sculpture

Just as Italian architects influenced their French counterparts, Italian painters had a profound influence on French artists. Recognizing the greatness of Italian painters in his day, King Louis XIV's minister of royal works, Jean Baptiste Colbert,

The Oath of the Horatii
by Jacques-Louis David

established the French Academy in Rome in 1666. French artists studied there under Italian masters at the king's expense. Colbert also founded France's Royal Academy of Painting and Sculpture.

In the years that followed, France produced numerous great painters of its own. Jacques-Louis David (1748–1825) became famous for his paintings with classical (Greek and Roman) themes, such as *The Oath of the Horatii* (1784) and *The Death of Socrates* (1787). In the 1800s, a romantic style of painting developed in France. Works in this style portrayed heroic, emotional, and dramatic themes. The chief French romantic painter was Eugène Delacroix (1798–1863), whose world-famous work *Liberty Leading the People* (1830) now hangs in the Louvre.

The second half of the nineteenth century witnessed the emergence of impressionism, a new and original French art

Claude Monet, Impressionist Master

Claude Monet was one of the founders and masters of the modern impressionist movement. He is famous for his river and garden scenes and also for painting a single object from several different viewpoints and at different times of day, reflecting varying lighting conditions. He settled in Giverny, on the Seine River west of Paris, and there installed a lily pond that became the subject of many of his works. His world-famous paintings of water lilies now hang in French museums, as well as in New York City's Metropolitan Museum of Art.

movement that subsequently influenced artists around the world. The impressionist style emphasizes feeling and texture rather than strict form and detail. A typical work gives a rough, sketchy, or soft-focus "impression" of a subject rather than a realistic depiction of it. Among the movement's founders were Pierre Auguste Renoir (1841–1919) and Claude Monet (1840–1926).

The Thinker by Auguste Rodin

The nineteenth century also produced France's greatest sculptor and indeed, one of the finest sculptors of all times—Auguste Rodin (1840–1917). Known primarily for working in bronze, an alloy (mixture) of the metals copper and tin, his most famous sculpture is probably *The Thinker*. But many art critics consider his depiction of two young lovers, *The Kiss*, completed in 1886, to be his masterpiece.

Inventor of High Fashion

Paris is the fashion capital of the world, where leading clothes designers present their new collections each year. The now globally popular industry of elegant, high-fashion clothes, which the French call *haute couture*, was invented in France in the 1850s. An Englishman named Charles Worth settled permanently in Paris and opened the first fashion salon. Later French designers, including Coco Chanel, Christian Dior, Pierre Cardin, and Yves Saint-Laurent, largely set the world's fashion standards in the twentieth century.

A Traditional Fascination for Ideas

French writers and their works have long ranked among the world's most brilliant and important. The French have a longstanding love of language, and France has produced many great intellectuals and writers. They also have a traditional fascination with ideas. Over the centuries, their literature has been a source of national pride and has often helped to shape their national identity. French writers have also set standards for writers in other countries. All the French works mentioned below strongly influenced the development of world literature and are still widely read and studied today.

The first literary works that can be termed uniquely French were medieval romantic tales of daring and heroic knights. The most famous is the *Chanson de Roland (Song of Roland)*. Composed by an unknown twelfth-century poet, it describes the exploits and death of one of Charlemagne's bravest knights, Sir Roland.

A Great Comic Playwright

Molière was the stage name adopted by the brilliant French actor-director-playwright Jean-Baptiste Poquelin. During his successful career, he wrote twelve of the greatest and funniest comedies of all time, including *Tartuffe* (1664), *The Doctor in Spite of Himself* (1666), and *The Imaginary Invalid* (1673). In the 1660s, Louis XIV, the Sun King, appointed Molière's theatrical troupe as an official provider of entertainment for the royal court.

In the 1600s, French literature flowered as never before, and that century is still seen as a literary golden age. The era's greatest tragic dramatists were Pierre Corneille (1606–1684) and Jean Racine (1639–1699). Humor was not neglected however, as Molière (1622–1673), one of the best comic playwrights who ever lived, turned out a string of hilarious masterpieces. The century also saw the emergence in France of the world's first modern philosopher, René Descartes (1596–1650). He tried to develop a method for discerning the truth about life and the world and is most famous for his statement "I think, therefore I am."

From the Enlightened to the Absurd

In the eighteenth century, France continued to introduce new, profound, and lasting ideas to the rest of the world. In an awakening spirit of scientific inquiry, thinkers and writers began to question everything, including concepts of government author-

Voltaire was part of the intellectual movement known as the French Enlightenment.

ity, freedom, and human rights. This intellectual movement, as well as the era, became known as the French Enlightenment. One particularly enlightened writer was the brilliant Voltaire (1694–1778). He compared the autocratic French monarchy to the more democratic British Parliament and concluded that the British system was better. Montesquieu (1689–1755) and Jean-Jacques Rousseau (1712–1778) also championed democratic ideals. Their writings strongly inspired the leaders of both the American and French Revolutions.

A succession of great novelists highlighted French literature in the 1800s. The master of the historical novel in this era was Victor Hugo (1802–1885). His *Hunchback of Notre Dame* (1831), about a deformed bell-ringer's love for a gypsy girl, effectively captured life in medieval Paris. In the hands of Gustave Flaubert (1821–1880), Émile Zola (1840–1902), and others, realistic contemporary novels also came of age. At the same time, Jules Verne (1828–1905) helped to pioneer the new literary genre of science fiction with

Émile Zola, Novelist and Humanitarian

French writer Émile Zola became famous for his realistic and often controversial novels, including *The Dram-Shop* (1877), *Nana* (1880), and *The Human Animal* (1890). These deal mostly with the everyday lives and problems of French working-class people in his era. Zola was also a champion of justice and human rights. His daring 1898 open letter to the nation's president, titled *J'accuse* (I Accuse), launched the campaign that eventually freed the falsely convicted Jewish army officer Alfred Dreyfus.

his popular novels *From the Earth to the Moon* (1865) and *Twenty Thousand Leagues under the Sea* (1870).

In the twentieth century, French writers continued to innovate and to influence their counterparts in other countries. Among the new, experimental, thought-provoking literary forms that emerged in France was existentialism. Existentialist writers, like Jean-Paul Sartre (1905–1980) in his play *No Exit* (1944) and Albert Camus (1913–1960) in *The Stranger* (1942), stressed life's more absurd and meaningless aspects.

Another important modern literary movement, the "theater of the absurd," emerged in Paris in the 1950s. Through their works, the absurdists argued that the nature of life and the world is beyond human understanding. The most famous absurdist play was *Waiting for Godot* (1953), by Samuel Beckett. Beckett was an Irishman who settled in Paris and wrote in French.

Music and Movies

France has also given the world some of its most splendid symphonic music. Hundreds of thousands of French, as well as many foreign visitors, flock each year to concert halls in Paris and other cities to hear the works of French composers. Perhaps the greatest of them all was the talented and influential Hector Berlioz (1803–1869). Many of his works, including the *Symphonie Fantastique* (1830) and *Harold in Italy* (1834), have become modern classics performed yearly around the world. His arrangement of France's national anthem is the finest ever created and remains one of his most popular

A caricature of Hector Berlioz leading an orchestra

compositions, especially in France. Another important French composer was Georges Bizet (1838–1875), who wrote the famous and tuneful opera *Carmen*.

When they are not strolling through museums, sitting in concert halls, or curling up with a good book, it is a good bet the French are at the movies. In fact, movies are so popular in France that the average person sees a film at least once a week. The tradition dates back to 1895. That year, in Paris, the

Lumière brothers, Louis and Auguste, inventors of the film projector, gave the world's first public screening of a motion picture. Since that time, France has produced hundreds of great film directors and actors. The most popular actor in recent years has been the hulking and hugely talented Gérard Dépardieu.

Unlike American films, which often emphasize action and spectacle, French movies tend to be smaller in scale and deal with human problems and relationships. But the French like American movies too, which they watch in English with French subtitles.

France's Biggest Movie Star

Gérard Dépardieu (1948–) has been France's most popular film actor for two decades. In trouble with the law while in his teens, he redeemed himself by taking up acting. Dépardieu is a stocky, tough-looking man with strong, expressive facial features. An extremely powerful and gifted actor, he has played a wide range of characters, including the title role in *Cyrano de Bergerac* (right, 1990), for which he won a César, the French version of the Oscar. He has also appeared in American films, including *Green Card* (1990) and *The Man in the Iron Mask* (1998).

At Home, at School, and at Play

THE AVERAGE FRENCH RESIDENCE HAS CHANGED A GREAT deal over the course of the twentieth century. This is partly because France lagged behind other industrialized countries in building large quantities of modern, affordable housing. As late as 1945, only 10 percent of all French homes had a bath or shower. And only about one in four had indoor flush toilets.

This situation improved when the government built hundreds of high-rise apartment buildings at the edges of cities in the late 1940s and 1950s. Such public housing was needed to accommodate the huge numbers of rural people then moving to the cities to take jobs in factories and businesses. These buildings were modern, with flush toilets and other conveniences, and rents were affordable.

But many French people did not like living in big apartment buildings. Though modern, the rooms were usually small. And there was not enough room for each family to have a personal garden, a luxury many former rural inhabitants had

Opposite: **Many French people enjoy fishing.**

A small apartment complex

come to take for granted. So large numbers of people began building private homes, a trend that contributed to the growth of sprawling suburbs around the cities. Today, close to 60 percent of the French live in private homes in either urban or rural areas. And many French people own more than one home. France has the world's highest proportion—13 percent—of families who own vacation homes. Most second homes are in quiet, country villages where their owners can escape the hustle and bustle of the cities.

Time Off

One thing all French people have in common, whether they live in apartments or private homes, in the city or the country, is an increasing amount of leisure time. The government recently reduced the workweek to thirty-eight hours. French workers get four or five weeks of paid vacation annually, and the legal retirement age is sixty, compared to sixty-five in the United States. There are also numerous holidays, both religious and secular (nonreligious).

France's National Holidays and Observances

Le Jour de l'An (New Year's Day)	January 1
Poisson d'avril (April Fools Day)	April 1
La fête des mères (Mother's Day)	A Sunday in May
La fête des pères (Father's Day)	A Sunday in June
La fête du travail (Labor Day)	May 1
La fête nationale (Independence Day)	July 14
L'Armistice (Armistice Day)	November 11

What do the French do with so much spare time? Studies show that they spend much of it watching television. Over 70 percent of French households have TV sets and the average family watches about three-and-a-half hours of television every day. By comparison, the average U.S. family spends about seven hours a day, or twice as long, in front of the tube. When not watching TV, many French people spend their leisure time reading or attending movies, concerts, plays, operas, museums, and sports events. The other most common pastimes include fishing, hunting, hiking, gardening, and doing household repairs.

Flowering plants adorn this stone cottage.

What and When the French Eat

The French also devote considerable time and attention to preparing and eating their meals. French cooking and French restaurants are world renowned. And indeed, the French consider a well-prepared, unhurried meal to be one of life's greatest pleasures.

This tradition has long included the famous gourmet cooking style the French call *haute cuisine* (high cooking). It is characterized by very rich foods made with lots of butter, cream, eggs, and expensive spices. Another cooking style—*la nouvelle cuisine* (new cooking)—has become increasingly popular in recent years. New cooking uses mostly lighter, lower-fat ingredients, especially vegetables and fruits. Fast-food shops, inspired by the American versions, have also gained popularity in France, particularly among young people. Borrowing the English term, the French refer to them as *le fast-food*.

Although many busy working people and students frequently grab some fast food to save time, most French people still prefer and look forward to home-cooked meals. In order to make sure the ingredients are as fresh as possible, the average family does at least some food shopping every day. Although there are large supermarkets, as in the United

Haute Cuisine

Surprisingly, the person who established traditional French *haute cuisine* was not French, but Italian. In 1600, France's King Henry IV asked an Italian princess named Maria de Médici to come to France and be his wife. Maria brought her own cooks with her and the rich dishes they prepared for the court caught on in most noble households. After the French Revolution, *haute cuisine* also became popular among the members of the lower classes.

States, most French people prefer to shop in small specialty stores. One of these is the *boucherie*, where a butcher cuts meats exactly as the customer requests. Another is the *crémerie*, where one can find a large variety of cheeses. Other specialty shops include the *charcuterie*, a deli that sells salads and meat pies, the *boulangerie*, or bakery, and the *pâtisserie*, or pastry shop.

A *boulangerie*, or bakery

A Typical Traditional Meal

Traditional French lunches and dinners have several courses, served one at a time. First comes the *hors d'oeuvres*, or appetizers. These usually consist of soups, salads, or light finger foods. Then comes the main course, most often some kind of meat and one or two vegetables. Some favorite combinations are chicken and fried potatoes (*poulet frites*), veal with rice (*blanquette de veau*), chicken in red wine (*coq au vin*) with boiled potatoes, and beef stew (*pot au feu*) with mixed vegetables. The third course might be salad (unless salad was an *hors d'oeuvre*). Diners then continue to the next course—creamy wedges of one or more of the hundreds of varieties of cheese made in France. Finally comes desert, usually some pastry, fruit, or yogurt. Wine is the traditional and still most common dinner drink, although mineral water and beer have become almost as popular.

The first meal of the day, breakfast, or *le petit déjeuner*, is most often quick and light. Usually it consists of some bread or a croissant, with butter and jam, washed down with a cup of coffee or tea. Lunch, or *le déjeuner*, used to be the day's main meal. However, it has recently been giving way to dinner, *le dîner*, mainly because workers' lunch hours are shorter now, allowing less time to enjoy lengthy noon meals. The exception is Sunday lunch, still customarily a leisurely meal in which family and friends gather to enjoy food and conversation.

Many French couples hold two separate marriage ceremonies. The civil ceremony is the required, legal one and usually takes place at the local city hall. If the couple desires a church ceremony too, it customarily follows the civil one. In France, getting married is not viewed as such a life-altering step as it is in the United States. However, having children *is* such a step to the French, because it brings heavy responsibilities and obligations.

Having children also establishes a family. In France, the family is by far the most important social unit. In fact, the government pays a monthly allowance to each family based on the number of children it has. Extended families, including grandparents, aunts, uncles, and cousins, are usually very closely knit and supportive and protective of each member. Quite often these large family units include pets—the French

A civil marriage ceremony

are avid animal lovers. France has the highest percentage of homes with pets in Europe. One out of three French homes has a dog, and in Paris there are more dogs than children.

Whether they grow up in extended families or not, French children receive a lot of supervision and guidance. The French view child-rearing as a serious and important job, and French parents and other relatives watch their children's behavior closely and are not shy about disciplining them in public. This is because adults feel it is their responsibility to civilize young people and help them become productive members of society. As a result, French children tend to be more mature and well behaved than American children of the same age.

French children tend to be well behaved.

Education

French children are usually better educated than young people in many other nations. This is partly because of the splendid cultural traditions and institutions that surround young people in France. It is also because French parents are very concerned with making sure their children study hard and get good grades. They know that those who do well in school often get the best jobs and make higher salaries later in life. It is also extremely important to the French, young and old alike, to appear literate, cultured, and well spoken, to avoid seeming uncivilized.

Another reason that French children tend to be well educated is that they put in long hours of study, in school and at home too. On average, school classes begin between 8:00 and 8:30 in the morning and end between 4:00 and 4:30 in the afternoon. When they get home, most students are expected to complete their homework before dinner. In many homes,

Doing homework

mothers supervise this work strictly. And although French students have numerous school vacations, they are assigned lengthy *devoirs de vacances*, "vacation homework."

Most French children attend *école maternelle*, or nursery school, before they are six years old. From ages six to eleven they go to primary school, after which they have four years of junior high, called *collège*. At age sixteen they can either quit school or pursue higher learning. Those who do go on enter a *lycée*, a high school that prepares them to take the *baccalauréat*, or "*bac*," a very difficult university entrance exam. Students who pass the bac (about one-third of them fail) enroll in one of France's more than seventy universities or in one of many *grandes écoles*—special colleges that prepare people for careers as politicians or lawyers. All forms of higher education in France are publicly financed and no tuition is charged.

Sports, in School and Out

Although French children study long and hard, they find ample time for leisure activities and enjoy sports. They play some sports at school, since French schools strongly encourage physical fitness, called *la forme*. During daily breaks from academic classes, students participate in volleyball, gymnastics, and soccer (which the French call football). Many schools also sponsor one-week stays at the seashore or in the mountains. On these retreats, students still attend classes, but also learn to swim or ski.

Despite the emphasis French schools place on them, sports are less of a national obsession in France than they are in the United States and Canada. In general, the French prefer playing

A Favorite Game

Many French boys and men enjoy playing the country's second-most popular team game, rugby. The game is played in backyards, in school playing fields, and also by professional teams in stadiums. A rugby ball is shaped somewhat like an American football. In fact, rugby is the direct ancestor of American football. The two games have a number of differences, however. Blocking and interference are illegal in rugby, so the players need no heavy padding, as American football players do. An amateur rugby team has fifteen players, while a professional team has thirteen. As in football, the object is to carry the ball over the opposing team's goal line, and players advance the ball by running with, passing, or kicking it. However, no forward passes are allowed in rugby. Also, rugby play is continuous, stopping only when the ball goes out of bounds or someone breaks a rule.

and watching individual sports, particularly skiing, cycling, and swimming, to team sports. Tennis, golf, and sailing are also popular. The main exceptions are two team sports played both in backyards and professionally—rugby and soccer. National soccer championships constitute one of France's three major yearly spectator events. The other two are the

The Tour de France

Every year in June and July the French hold one of their most popular and famous sporting events, the Tour de France. Huge crowds watch hundreds of cyclists race madly across the countryside. The grueling competition lasts twenty-six days and covers 2,455 miles (3,950 km). The winner receives international acclaim.

Tour de France, an exciting cross-country bicycle race, and the Grand Prix car races held at Le Mans, about 117 miles (188 km) southwest of Paris.

Communication, with Words and Without

Of the many aspects of life in France that are uniquely French, the way the people communicate, both verbally and nonverbally, is one of the most distinctive. They follow certain verbal rules of etiquette that sometimes appear strange to foreigners, but they expect visitors to at least try to follow the most fundamental of such rules. When entering a shop, for example, you are expected to say hello (*bonjour*) to the owner or clerk, and in fact it is considered rude not to do so. Likewise, you should say thank you (*merci*) and good-bye (*au revoir*) when leaving the shop, even if no sale took place.

The French also consider conversation to be both a skill and an art. Often their conversations escalate into what foreigners view as heated arguments. But such exchanges are rarely angry or violent. They are better described as "spirited but friendly" attempts to exchange opinions. Besides, they follow certain rules that all French people know and accept as polite and civil.

The most important rule of conversation in France is to choose an acceptable topic. The French seldom, if ever, engage in idle chatter about the weather or their personal problems, and they consider visitors who do engage in such chatter to be shallow, or boring, or both. They particularly frown on discussing money casually and consider it impolite to ask someone what they do to make their money. This is because the French consider it vulgar to talk about money openly. Visitors to France need to remember *not* to ask the natives what they do for a living. More common and accepted topics of conversation in France are national and world politics, which foods and wines are best, and the merits of specific artists, singers, and actors. In other words, the topic should have substance and be worth arguing about.

Nonverbal communication is just as important as the verbal kind in France. And foreign visitors sometimes unknowingly create distrust or offense by using the wrong gesture or facial expression. Smiling is a common example. Americans tend to smile a lot when traveling abroad, assuming it is a universal sign of friendliness. In France, however, smiling without a good reason, especially at a stranger, is often viewed as unpleasant, suspicious, or even idiotic. The French enjoy smiling, but usually wait until they feel there is a good reason to do so.

Timeline

French History		World History	
Celtic tribes migrate from central Europe into France.	c. 1000–750 B.C.	Egyptians build the Pyramids and Sphinx in Giza.	2500 B.C.
A group of Celts found a fishing village that will later become Paris.	c. 250 B.C.	Buddha is born in India.	563 B.C.
Julius Caesar conquers Gaul (France); Gaul subsequently becomes a Roman province.	58–52 B.C.		
French leader Charles Martel defeats an invading Muslim army at Tours.	A.D. 732	The Roman emperor Constantine recognizes Christianity.	A.D. 313
Charles Martel's grandson, Charlemagne, is crowned emperor.	800	The prophet Muhammad begins preaching a new religion called Islam.	610
French duke William of Normandy defeats the English in the battle of Hastings.	1066	The Eastern (Orthodox) and Western (Roman) Churches break apart.	1054
		William the Conqueror defeats the English in the Battle of Hastings.	1066
		Pope Urban II proclaims the First Crusade.	1095
		King John seals the Magna Carta.	1215
The French are defeated by the English at Crécy, in northern France.	1346	The Renaissance begins in Italy.	1300s
French maiden Joan of Arc raises the siege of Orléans.	1429	The Black Death sweeps through Europe.	1347
King Charles VII drives the English out of France.	1453	Ottoman Turks capture Constantinople, conquering the Byzantine Empire.	1453
		Columbus arrives in North America.	1492
French explorer Jacques Cartier makes his first voyage to Canada.	1534	The Reformation leads to the birth of Protestantism.	1500s
Louis XIV, the "Sun King," rules France.	1643–1715		

French History		World History	
France fights England in the Seven Years' War (also called the French and Indian War).	1756–1763		
		1776	The Declaration of Independence is signed.
The French Revolution begins; the Bastille falls on July 14.	1789	1789	The French Revolution begins.
Napoléon becomes dictator of France.	1799		
Napoléon is defeated at Waterloo.	1815		
The French establish the Second Republic.	1848		
		1865	The American Civil War ends.
Diggers find the remains of early humans in Cro-Magnon, southern France.	1868		
The French establish the Third Republic.	1870		
France enters World War I.	1914	1914	World War I breaks out.
		1917	The Bolshevik Revolution brings Communism to Russia.
		1929	Worldwide economic depression begins.
		1939	World War II begins, following the German invasion of Poland.
German Nazis invade and occupy France in World War II.	1940		
The French establish the Fourth Republic.	1946		
France joins Europe's Common Market.	1957	1957	The Vietnam War starts.
The French establish the Fifth Republic.	1958		
France grants Algeria its independence.	1962		
France creates first national park, the Vanoise.	1963		
François Mitterand is elected president of France.	1981		
France helps form the European Union.	1992		
		1989	The Berlin Wall is torn down as Communism crumbles in Eastern Europe.
A tunnel under the English Channel links France and England.	1994		
French voters choose Jacques Chirac as their president.	1995		
		1996	Bill Clinton is reelected U.S. president.

Fast Facts

Official name:	French Republic
Capital:	Paris
Official language:	French
Official religion:	None

Lyon

FRANCE
- Cities of over 150,000 people
- Smaller cities and towns
- Canals

0   100 miles
0   150 kilometers

French flag

Vanoise National Park

Nice

National anthem:	*"La Marseillaise"*
Type of government:	Democratic republic
Chief of state:	President
Head of government:	Prime minister
Area (including Corsica):	212,918 square miles (551,415 sq km)
Coordinates of geographic center:	46° 00' N, 2° 00' E
Dimensions:	North-south, 590 miles (950 km)
	East-west, 605 miles (974 km)
Bordering countries:	France borders Spain and Andorra in the south; Italy, Switzerland, and Germany in the east; and Luxembourg and Belgium in the northeast.
Highest elevation:	Mont Blanc, 15,771 feet (4,807 m)
Lowest elevation:	Sections of the delta of the Rhône River that are slightly below sea level.
Average temperature:	Paris: 75°F (24°C) in July, 43°F (6°C) in January
	Nice: 81°F (27°C) in July, 55°F (13°C) in January
Average annual rainfall:	Brest (Atlantic seaboard), 45 inches (114 cm); Marseille (Mediterranean coast), 22 inches (56 cm)
National population:	58,804,944 (1998 est.)

Population of largest cities (1990 est):

Paris	2,175,200
Marseille	807,726
Lyon	422,444
Toulouse	365,933
Nice	345,674

Eiffel Tower

Currency

Famous landmarks:
- ▶ *Eiffel Tower* (Paris)
- ▶ *Louvre* (Paris)
- ▶ *Cathedral of Notre Dame* (Paris)
- ▶ *Palace of Versailles* (Versailles)
- ▶ *Mont-St-Michel* (borders Normandy and Brittany)
- ▶ *Omaha Beach* (Normandy)

Industry: France has a diverse mix of industries. It mines coal, natural gas, iron, bauxite, potash, and other natural substances and uses these to manufacture steel, aluminum, cars, ships, airplanes, chemicals, fertilizers, and other useful products. The world's fourth-largest exporter, it ships almost $300 billion worth of goods to other countries each year. France is also the second-largest exporter of farm products in the world. Its major agricultural products are wheat, sugar beets, corn (maize), beef, poultry, milk, and wine.

Currency: France's basic unit of currency is the franc. In 1999, U.S.$1 = 6.23 francs.

Weights and measures: Metric system

Literacy: 99%

Common words and phrases:

Adieu, or *Au revoir.*	Good-bye.
Bonjour.	Hello *or* Good day.
C'est la vie.	That's life.
Comment ça va?	How are you?
crème de la crème	the best
déjà vu	the feeling you have seen something before
De rien.	You're welcome.
Enchanté.	Pleased to meet you *or* I'm delighted.

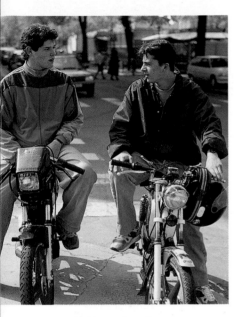

Taking a break

esprit de corps	group spirit
Excusez-moi.	Excuse me.
faux pas	a mistake
Je m'appelle . . .	My name is . . .
joie de vivre	joy in being alive
Merci.	Thank-you.
non	no
oui	yes
pardon	sorry
Parlez-vous anglais?	Do you speak English?
raison d'être	a reason for existing
s'il vous plaît	please
Voilà.	There you have it.

Famous French people:

Napoléon Bonaparte *Emperor*	(1769–1821)
John Calvin *Religious leader*	(1509–1564)
Jacques Cartier *Explorer*	(1491–1557)
Charlemagne *Ruler*	(742–814)
Jacques Chirac *President*	(1932–)
Charles de Gaulle *Military leader, president*	(1890–1970)
Victor Hugo *Writer*	(1802–1885)
Joan of Arc *Saint, national heroine*	(1412–1431)
Louis XIV *King*	(1638–1715)
Claude Monet *Painter*	(1840–1926)
Pierre Auguste Renoir *Painter*	(1841–1919)
Vercingetorix *Military leader*	(?–46 B.C.)

Jacques Chirac

To Find Out More

Nonfiction

▶ Daley, Robert. *Portraits of France.* Boston: Little, Brown, 1991.

▶ Jones, Colin. *The Cambridge Illustrated History of France.* New York: Cambridge University Press, 1994.

▶ MacKendrick, Paul. *Roman France.* New York: St. Martin's Press, 1972.

▶ Nardo, Don. *Caesar's Conquest of Gaul.* San Diego: Lucent Books, 1996.

▶ Nardo, Don. *The Trial of Joan of Arc.* San Diego: Lucent Books, 1998.

▶ Nardo, Don. *The French Revolution.* San Diego: Greenhaven Press, 1999.

▶ Price, Roger. *A Concise History of France.* New York: Cambridge University Press, 1993.

▶ Taylor, Sally A. *Culture Shock! France: A Guide to Customs and Etiquette.* Portland, OR: Graphic Arts Center Publishing, 1990.

Videotapes

▶ *Romantic France: Paris and the Loire Valley* (1995, Maier Communications). A travelogue highlighting the attractions of Paris and central France.

▶ *The Hunchback of Notre Dame* (1939, RKO). The best of many film versions of Victor Hugo's classic novel about Quasimodo, a deformed bell-ringer who gives a gypsy girl sanctuary in the famous Paris cathedral.

▶ *An American in Paris* (1951, MGM-UA). Sparkling musical comedy romp, starring Gene Kelly and set in the French capital. Recently voted one of the top 100 American films.

▶ *Paths of Glory* (1957, MGM-UA). Stanley Kubrick's great antiwar film, starring Kirk Douglas and depicting gruesome trench warfare in France during World War I.

- *Jean de Florette* (1986, Orion). Director Claude Berri embroiders a richly textured and emotional story of provincial French farm and village life.

- *Les Miserables* (1996, Warner Brothers). This updated rendition of Victor's Hugo's classic tale of a petty thief relentlessly hunted by a lawman is beautifully acted, suspenseful, and riveting.

Websites

- **American Embassy in Paris**
  http://www.amb-usa.fr/
  Provides economic and other information about France of interest to Americans and Canadians planning to visit or already in France.

- **The French Connection**
  http://members.mint.net/frenchcx/index.html
  A collection of links to websites providing information about French places and cultural and sports events.

- **Practical France, The Practical Information Link**
  http://www.visiteurope.com/france/France03.htm
  Displays tourist information on France such as attractions, activities, and geography.

- **Paris**
  http://www.paris.org/
  A grab bag of information on the city's monuments, museums, stores, hotels, restaurants, and more.

- **French Historical Text Archive**
  http://www.geocities.com/Athens/Forum/9061/europe/france.html
  Provides information about French history and culture, including texts of original French documents.

- **La Marseillaise**
  http://www.adminet.com/marseillaise.html
  Provides sheet music, audio files, and lyrics, in both French and English, for France's stirring national anthem.

Organizations and Embassies

- **French Embassy**
  4101 Reservoir Rd., N.W.
  Washington, DC 20007
  (202) 944-6000

- **French Government Tourist Office**
  8 avenue de l'Opera
  75001 Paris
  France
  01-42-96-10-23

Index

Page numbers in *italics* indicate illustrations.

holidays
national, 116
religious, 101
hornbeam tree, 35–36
Hôtel de Ville (City Hall), 63
housing, 82, 115–116, 115, 117
Hugo, Victor, 110, 133
Huguenots, 95, 95
Hunchback of Notre Dame
(Victor Hugo), 110
Hundred Years' War, 47
map of, 47

I

immigration, 85
insect life, 36–37
Institutes of the Christian Religion
(John Calvin), 96
Introduction to a Devout Life
(Francis de Sales), 93
Isère River, 27
Islamic religion, 86, 99

J

Joan of Arc, 8, 12–13, 93, 133
Joan of Arc Led to Her Execution
(Isidor Patrois), 13
Judaism, 96–98
judicial branch (of government), 64

L

language, 87–89
Breton dialect, 89
franglais dialect, 89
nonverbal communication, 127
Provençal dialect, 89
rules of etiquette, 88, 126–127
Lascaux cave paintings, 40, 40
Le Nôtre, André, 50
Le Vau, Louis, 50

legislative branch (of government),
64–66
Leo III (pope), 45
literature, 108–109
Hunchback of Notre Dame
(Victor Hugo), 110
Institutes of the Christian Religion
(John Calvin), 96
Introduction to a Devout Life
(Francis de Sales), 93
No Exit (Jean-Paul Sartre), 111
Song of Roland (author unknown),
108
The Stranger (Albert Camus), 111
livestock, 19, 25, 31, 37, 37, 71, 80
local government, 68. See also
government; regional government.
Loire River, 17
Lorraine region, 89
Louis XIV, King of France, 49, 49,
105, 133
Louis XV, King of France, 51
Louis XVI, King of France, 51–52
Louvre, 102, 104–105
Lumière, Auguste, 113
Lumière, Louis, 113
Luxembourg Gardens, 58
Lyon, 20, 20, 83

M

manufacturing, 71, 72, 77–79, 85
maps. See also historical maps.
geopolitical, 11
natural resources, 78
Paris, 63
population distribution, 83
regional governments, 67
topographical, 19
maritime pine trees, 36
marriage, 121, 121
The Marseillaise (national anthem),
69, 111

Marseille
climate of, 23
population of, 83
Martel, Charles, 45
Massif Central, 23–25, 24, 78, 82, 83
Massilia, 42
de Médici, Maria, 118
Mediterranean Sea, 22
Merovingian dynasty, 44–45
Mesozoic Era, 25
mining, 71, 77–79, 77
Ministry for the Environment and
the Quality of Life, 33
Mitterrand, François, 62, 64
Molière (Jean-Baptiste Poquelin),
109, 109
Mona Lisa (Leonardo da Vinci), 104
Monet, Claude, 107, 133
Mont Blanc, 27, 27
Montesquieu, 110
Montpellier, 68
music, 69, 111–113, 112
Muslim population, 86–87, 98,
98, 100

N

Napoléon III, King of France, 54
Narbonese province, 42
national anthem (The Marseillaise),
69, 111
National Assembly, 51, 65, 65
national flag, 61, 61
National Forest Service, 32
National Front Party, 87, 100
national holidays, 51, 51, 116
national parks, 33–34
natural resources map, 78
nature preserves, 34
Neanderthals, 39
new cooking, 118

Meet the Author

Don Nardo is a historian and award-winning writer who specializes in ancient Greek and Roman civilizations. He has traveled widely in Europe and studied firsthand many of the ancient sites he writes about. One of his many books about the ancient world is *Caesar's Conquest of Gaul*, about the first Roman incursions into the area that later became France. Fascinated by later historical periods as well, he has also published books about Joan of Arc and the French Revolution.

"It was my interest in Roman France, Joan's exploits, and the turbulent revolutionary period," he says, "that made me decide to do this book about France for the Enchantment of the World series. Building on my knowledge of these phases of French history, I consulted several noted French history texts, as well as a number of volumes about the country's geography,

culture, and customs. Almanacs, encyclopedias, travel guides, Internet websites, and telephone calls and faxes to French embassies and cultural organizations also provided much useful information. During these researches, it came in handy that I am able to read and speak a little French."

Mr. Nardo grew up in Massachusetts. He studied theater at Syracuse University and made his living for some years as an actor before returning to college to get his history degree. He then taught high school for eight years, while writing part-time, before finally devoting himself completely to writing in the mid-1980s. Since that time he has published over 100 books, many of them for student use. He has also written several screenplays and teleplays, including work for ABC-TV. Mr. Nardo resides with his wife Christine on Cape Cod, Massachusetts.

Photo Credits